ANCIENT BLOOD OF VIOLENCE

Humanity's history of sin that brought hatred,
violence and death.

by
John Bazzanella

Copyright

John Bazzanella
bazzanella413@yahoo.com.ph
www.johnbazzanellabooks.com
Printed in the United States of America

AUTHOR'S FOREWORD

PART I

Our planet earth is now blue because of thousands of years of a violent history to the present that has infiltrated our conscience and put a knife in the heart of the innocent victims of violence. At the time of this writing today at the beginning of March / 2023 and as I write through the journey of this book more violence will happen on this planet as I write. We are our own prophets who are inspired by common occurrences of our present-day violence so much so that life itself has become our tomb. This book is dedicated to the memory of all the Police officers who gave up their lives to protect us in the face of a depraved and corrupt planet that is harboring the evil side of humanity. And also, to the Firefighters, Aviation Pilots and Police Officers and Military Peace Keepers who were victims of terrorism. If the names of all these heroes were mentioned in this book, I would need to add another thousand pages filled with the names of the Police Officers, Firefighters, Aviation Pilots, Paramedics, and Doctors and Nurses, Military soldiers and personnel and humanity's workers of charities throughout the world who gave up their lives in the war zones. Where these war zones have destroyed peaceful communities. May we find peace in a barbaric and war-torn world filled with and plagued by the Ancient Blood of Violence! Because of the violence that has been done to the innocent and to the heroes who lost their lives. Where the stories here have to be told without concealing the disturbing content of these stories. My argument here is why should we conceal these disturbing stories only for these violent perpetrators to win while the innocence of humanity has to keep silent?

AUTHOR'S FOREWORD
PART II

The image of the skull on the cover of this book with a dagger going through it; is a symbolic message of violence with a weapon, and that it is also a symbolic message of the dagger going through the brain representing the evil of the spiritual character of mankind's sins of adultery and fornication and excessive lust and murder. Where the dagger going through the skull and brain represents the harm humanity is doing to itself by all these different sins of hatred and violence and lust and murder. Turning the soul and spirit into a depraved and despicable state of corruption that inflicts harm to humanity by violence and / or physical corruption of the flesh by these sins of hatred and violence and lust and murder that leads to murder and death by the genocides perpetrated on this planet that has happened or will eventually happen in the future. Since the brain in the skull is the partial workings of the soul and spirit according to Galatians 5: 16, 17, 18, 19, 20, 21.

CONTENTS

ABOUT THE AUTHOR

John Bazzanella has written four previous books. His first book was entitled "Pyromancy." His second book was a compilation of three short books entitled "Open Tomb, Aviation 666, Monsters of Genesis." His third book was entitled "Magistrates of Damnation" which is a serious and briefly revised version of his first book "Pyromancy." Also, a fourth book that is also in the process of being published called "Immunity From Prosecution." All these four books were inspired by an encounter with a seal or message from God that happened on Friday August 12th / 1983. After this seal or message from God, a violent act of attempted murder on a police officer took place on October 2nd / 1983 where he rammed a police cruiser. Where here no one got hurt in this crime or offence he committed. He had no criminal or psychiatric record prior to this crime or offence of attempted murder on this police officer. He was then found not guilty by reason of insanity on June 11th / 1984, because of revealing that he was sealed by God and was then incarcerated in psychiatric institutions. After this crime and conviction of this crime he spent close to the next 40 years incarcerated in and out of psychiatric institutions and being at the same time under persecution. And still to this day on March 10th / 2023 after close to 40 years from 1983 to 2023 he is still incarcerated.

INTRODUCTION

There are "6" chapters in this book that symbolize the beginning of violence and the coming dawn of a depraved human civilization mentioned in Genesis 6: 5. The number "6" in Biblical numerical symbolism refers to "man" and the number "6" refers to evil which may also refer to "man" and the sinful nature that man had inherited by the first sin that infiltrated the human race. Here the first sin that was committed by Eve in this time period of Genesis, had spread when the fall of man into sin had occurred and that was committed in the human race for the very first time by Eve. And that this very first sin was the first temptation of sin by Eve that was first brought in. And that this first sign of iniquity was also the introduction of the beginning infiltration of wickedness into the human race in the time period of Genesis according to Genesis 3 : 1, 2, 3, 4, 5, 6, 7.

Evidence is vague in this book which is based on Biblical scripture and its related topics in research. If I burn or not in that furnace my books would sell perhaps millions of copies -- but as of now my books are not selling. Or as of now I have not been told by any of my publishers now for a year and 3 months how many copies have been sold of my books "Pyromancy" "Open Tomb, Aviation 666, Monsters of Genesis," "Magistrates of Damnation" at the time of this writing of March/ 2023 and going back to January / 2022. Since all my treasures or royalties of my books have possibly been taken by the U.S. and Canadian Government or known as Babylon which refers to the secularism of the world according to Isaiah 39: 1, 2, 3, 4, 5, 6, 7, 8.

 Also being sentenced to that furnace by the tyrants of this coming One World Government would be done in secrecy. So, if or when this furnace Judgment comes, this secrecy would eventually leak and be difficult to keep this conviction classified of a furnace that is a form of barbaric Ancient Blood of Violence in our present world of belligerence and hatred in the International Court of Justice of the United Nations under the rule and dictatorship of the of the office of the Anti-Christ and his colleagues who are the adversaries of the President of Ukraine Volodymyr Zelensky and who are also my adversaries that are mentioned in chapters 5 and 6 of this book " Ancient Blood of Violence."

Here once this classified information leaks out slowly or is revealed openly to the public and media worldwide then perhaps millions of copies of my books that I have written and had published will be sold. Here the International Court of Justice of the United Nations has a function that has a role to settle in accordance with International law, legal disputes submitted to it by states and give advisory opinions on legal questions referred to it by authorized United Nations organs and specialized agencies who may take advice and recommendations from the 10 Kings of the Global worldwide dictators and authoritarian regimes around the world in a coming future one world tyrannical government. Who may be involved with the Beast or Anti-Christ that will take my written rhetoric in my books of the Judgments of the Authorized King James Version Bible in accordance with their Apostate Religious beliefs seriously.

 And may make false claims that there will be peace coming through their own devices and further claim that I am destroying their efforts to bring peace in the world causing the perdition of civilization through my books and spreading false Biblical rhetoric? Is this all true? According to John 17: 12? And that I as a virgin of Israel had done a very horrible thing by writing these Books on the Bible like "Pyromancy" and "Open Tomb, Aviation 666, Monsters of Genesis" and "Magistrates of Damnation" and "Immunity from Prosecution" and this book "Ancient Blood of Violence" according to Jeremiah 18: 13. Also writing all these letters and e-mails to the media and Celebrities and Journalists and Reporters and News Anchors while being in a mental institution or this mental institution being the cold flowing waters that come from another place to be forsaken? According to Jeremiah 18: 13, 14, 15. But is this all true? Is it true of forsaking a servant of God and instead to believe in their own prophets who claim peace whom God had not sent these prophets. And where God says that there is no peace according to Jeremiah 14: 19 and also according to: Revelation 17: 12, 13 and Jeremiah 14:10, 11, 12, 13, 14, 15, 16.

Here this book "Ancient Blood of Violence" mentions is not only murder but torture that has survived through centuries by those who profess that they know God when in fact they are not true to God but reprobates according to Titus 1:16. Here they are assuming they are doing God service taking upon themselves the Judgments of God who are the political adversaries involved in this One World Government leader of the office of the Antichrist and their Apostate Religious ordinances and beliefs as mentioned in Chapter 5 and 6 of this book and their intentions of committing this worldwide genocide of these true Christians and their converts who are faithful to the Authorized King James Version Bible and where this genocide is carried out by a guillotine in a courtroom community district for refusing to swear allegiance to their One World Government in each and every community district courtroom, in each and every country where they receive a judgment sentence of execution in their own community in a courtroom on a guillotine in their community and other communities on a worldwide scale. For refusing to swear allegiance and refusing the Mark of the Beast of this One World Government according to John 16: 2 and Revelation 20: 4.

Also Christ not being with you but not going away expecting salvation from that individual because of the Ancient Blood of Violence that has survived down history, the barbaric Judgments of persecution down the centuries which is devastating torture which is not expedient, since there is no comfort in the Ancient Blood of Violence that is not only murder but torture in some cases that is done by men who are tyrants according to John 16: 7. Here they follow their precarious ways thinking they are doing God service in their Churches of Apostate Christianity according to John 16: 2 . Where they Judge the true Christian martyrs and converts of Christ and servants of God by a Furnace or Guillotines worldwide according to Matthew 13: 40, 41, 42 and Revelation 20: 4 and Revelation 6: 9, 10, 11 and Revelation 17: 5, 6. So those true Christians who are saved by drinking the Blood and water of Christ in order to get the Holy Spirit in them gets this comforter spoken of in John 16: 7, 8 and at this point having the privilege to being expedient who are the chaste virgins or the real pure virgins who are permitted to take the Mark of the Beast being not bond but free according to Revelation

13: 16. Then there are those who go in the rapture of saints according to 1st Thessalonians 4: 15, 16, 17 who are being caught up to heaven who had intercourse with multiple sexual partners here on earth not being a chaste virgin or not being a real pure virgin according to 1st Corinthians 7: 19, 20, 21, 22, 23, 33. Then also here there are the real meek of the earth who are the chaste virgins and the real pure virgins who do not go in that rapture of saints, but inherit the earth according to Matthew 5: 5 and Revelation 14: 4, 5. Getting this victory of salvation avoiding martyrdom by the Anti-Christ and the last plagues of Armageddon according to Revelation 9: 4, 5, 6 and Revelation 15: 1, 2, 3.

Here the Ancient Blood of Violence of a furnace is strictly a judgment scenario or purpose of God's prophetic destiny that is strictly for those who committed horrific sins of mass murders that have taken place in our societies like the mass shootings or the serial killers who have committed multiple murders that have offended humanity. Where here these offenders of these mass murders are gathered out of the Kingdom of Christ at the consummation of this age or the end of this world who refuse to worship the Anti-Christ or the beast and refuse to accept the Global I.D. or mark of the beast. And in the end being sentence to a furnace for refusing to swear allegiance to the Anti-Christ and accepting this Global registration I.D. or known also as the mark of the beast according to Matthew 13: 40, 41, 42 and be delivered from hell or the Lake of fire of Revelation 20: 12, 13, 14, 15, and be delivered from hell and the lake of fire according to 1st Corinthians 11: 31,32.

The following chapters of this book "Ancient Blood of Violence" reveals the history of the Ancient Blood of Violence and the crimes committed by these people of history. Also, the persecution of Christians or of the secular people who have been victims of murder or victims of crime going back to the past of the decades that had primitive laws. Resulting in more strict laws of convictions and sentences due to these primitive laws and their concluding consequences of more severe and strict convictions and punishments. Also, where this book "Ancient Blood of Violence" goes back centuries to the time of Christ where the laws back then had severe sentences and punishment for venial sins. That may have been unfortunately committed at the ancient times of blood and violent laws of convictions and punishments such as the ancient convictions sentences to the cross. And although it may be that there are perhaps no records of these conviction sentences to a cross and therefore, I made no mention in this book regarding these cruel punishments of the cross by ancient laws during the time of Christ.

CHAPTER 1
NEANDERTHAL CRIME

At El Sidron in Northern Spain Scientists have found evidence pointing to the cannibalism of 12 individuals by what is hypothesized to have been a neighboring group of Neanderthals. According to Carle Lalueza- Fox of the institute of evolutionary biology in Barcelona the individuals which were children aged from two to nine, and three teenagers and six adults appear to have been killed and eaten, with their bones and skulls split open to extract the marrow, tongue and brains. Scientists speculate that the lack of any evidence of fire makes it likely that the event of these killings and cannibalism happened in the winter, during a time when food was difficult to find or hunt for.

Evidence indicating that cannibalism would not make today's humans any different since we have been known today to have also practiced cannibalism or mortuary defleshing by birds or by other animals of wild life on a human body. Neanderthal are thought to have practiced cannibalism or ritual defleshing. This hypothesis was formulated after researchers found marks on Neanderthal bones similar to the bones of a dead deer butchered by Neanderthals. In 2020 a 50,000-year-old three ply cord fragment made bark was found at the Abri Du Maras France site. Bruce hardy of Kenyon College Ohio concluded that the creation of the cord suggested cognitive understanding of numeracy and context sensitive operational memory.

Here this primitive intellect would suggest that the Neanderthal was capable of being a cannibal and violent as well towards their peers because this intellect that creates an advantage against those peers who fail to devise or understand this cognitive understanding of numeracy and context sensitive operational memory. Which in the end brings about conflict or violence that may lead to murder because of a savage greed that these Neanderthal possessed among themselves.

This violence among Neanderthal is evident because of a 40,000-year-old Neanderthal skull of St. Cesaire that has a healed fracture in its cranial vault likely caused by something sharp, suggesting inter-personal violence. This wound healed and the Neanderthal survived. Neanderthal women appear to heavily skew physically impressive Neanderthal men hinting that Neanderthal men would compete with each other and polyamorous relationships would emerge that may cause violence competing for that attractive mate. We have this same mentality today in our society.

Also going back to the Sons of God or extraterrestrial entities or angels in and according to Genesis 6: 1, 2 and Jude 6? Is that they were the ones who mated with the ancient earthly daughters of men on this planet back in the time of Genesis. Not only was this mating forbidden by God but these earthly daughters or humans in general may have also had sexual relations or have been hunted and / or raped and / or been eaten by the Neanderthal species that is of the human variant specie of the Homo Sapiens. Furthermore, corrupting human flesh down the generations by these sexual sins before or after the Sons of God came to visit this planet going back to the time of Genesis. This was one of the reasons why man became so depraved in his physical appearance as well as in character. There is also ample evidence that supports this interbreeding between Homo Sapiens and the Neanderthal.

Having said this interbreeding may have reduced this life expectancy to the age of 35 for the Neanderthal. Where this interbreeding between the Neanderthal and Homo Sapiens and the further mating between the Sons of God and the daughters of men may have caused even more severe corruption to human flesh eventually down the centuries in our history to the present. This corruption consists of deformed birth defects and also being plagued by genetic or DNA flaws in the flesh bringing on disease of every sort including mental disorders.

Here because of the sins of mankind where mating with a variant specie like the Neanderthal they may have not been compatible in this mating with the Homo Sapiens specie or mating with a completely different being of origin from another part of the cosmos like an immortal being or extraterrestrial being or angel known also as the Sons of God that genetically may have not been compatible physically in this mating that brought on these plagues of sicknesses like diseases of every kind like Cancer, Diabetes, Heart Disease, Dementia, Parkinsons, Alzheimer's disease, multiple sclerosis, epilepsy, Aids, HIV, etc. where some of these diseases are not detected early enough where they possess a person early on as a pestilence undetected that walks in darkness according to Psalms 91: 6, 7, 8, 9, 10. Which brings on early death according to Galatians 6: 8.

So here the Sons of God have mated with the earthly daughters of men who were considered to be Homo Sapiens and these Homo Sapiens may have mated with the Neanderthal that may have not had a soul being a variant specie of the Homo Sapiens or the human entity created in the image of God that does have a soul according to Genesis 2: 7. Furthermore the Neanderthal were not the gentle, almost-human creatures portrayed in the media over the last 50 years or so. New Australian research reveals they were aggressive, powerful and terrifying carnivores --- ruthless and efficient apex predators or the most dangerous and successful predators of the human race who hunted, raped and ate early humans or early Homo Sapiens for over 50,000 years, perhaps before the visitation of the Sons of God to planet earth.

 The Neanderthal's daily diet of nearly 2kg of meat --the equivalent of 16 Quarter pounders --- included human flesh. Eurasian Neanderthals hunted, killed and cannibalized early humans for 50,000 years in an area of the Middle East known as the Mediterranean Levant. Because the two species of one being a Neanderthal and the other a Homo Sapiens were also variants to each other and they were possibly not sexually compatible. Eurasian Neanderthals also abducted and raped human females. This prolonged period of cannibalistic and sexual predation began about 100,000 years ago and that by 50,000 years ago, the human population in the Levant was reduced to as few as 50 individuals.

The death toll from the Neanderthal predation on Homo Sapiens generated the selection pressure for rebellion by humans against the Neanderthal. That transformed the tiny survivor population of early humans into modern humans today. With the intellect and means to develop and perform successful and victorious acts of violence due to prevalent results by the Neanderthal of war against their human adversaries. Who were the Neanderthal in the era of the Neanderthal period resulting into modern humans that have generated rebellion due to the violent acts of the Neanderthal against humans.

Who became capable of advance warfare in weaponry and violent behaviours resulting in worldwide wars and violence and societal conflicts in today's world. That is also now presently to date in our world that is filled with on-going violence in our communities and societies worldwide and war in other countries and in between and among rival countries themselves where this violence is also taking place as well. This ancient time of this Neanderthal conflict between the Neanderthal and this Levantine group of 50 individuals of humans or hominids that were victorious in this conflict survived and became the founding population of all humans living today in this violent and perilous times of the last days before the second coming of Christ according to 2nd Timothy 3: 1, 2, 3, 4, 5.

Also, there is an interesting paper by Julia Drell (2000: Neanderthals: a history of interpretation) That looks at how portrayals of Neanderthal have changed over time, as more evidence has become available --- and also as societal attitudes have changed, also note well, since it may well not be open-access. Drell also notes that suggestions of cannibalism by the Neanderthal are nothing new, first appearing in the 1860's. She cites an earlier author as saying that: there is not more universally common way of distancing from other people than to call them cannibals." In fact, there is not a lot of evidence of cannibalism in Neanderthals -- the remains of about 15 individuals that may have been eaten by their conspecifics or of the same specie. And over the span of their existence. Here Julia Drell is merely suggesting that cannibalism may have been not part of their diet or suggesting that they were good hunters and successful at large game. But Cannibalism here having a small amount of incidental evidence may refer that this cannibalism that was ether evident or not at all evident may suggest that this cannibalism among the Neanderthals themselves could have been violent incidents between themselves that had occurred.

Based on the research, Australian independent scholar Danny Vendramini has developed "Neanderthal predation theory," which argues that the evolution of modern humans --- including our unique physiology, sexuality and human nature -- is the result of a reaction to this systematic long -term sexual predation and cannibalism by Eurasian Neanderthals. Vendramini's forthcoming book "Them and Us": how Neanderthal predation created modern human's urges to fight back and describes how the human population of the Mediterranean Levant -- the population from which every human on earth is descended; and possibly originated from the Garden of Eden. Who were the descendants of Adam and Eve in this mix of the descendants in the ancient historical generations of these Biblical ages of these generations dating back to the time of Genesis and hundreds of thousands of years before the book of Genesis was written.

Here the Beginning of God's creation did not start a mere short 6 or 7 thousand years ago but hundreds of thousands if not millions of years before the five books of Moses of Genesis, Exodus, Leviticus, Numbers, Deuteronomy of the Bible of the Old Testament were written. Here Danny Vendramini has developed "The Neanderthal predation theory" that this theory is perhaps true to some point since I pointed out that humans were also sexually involved with the Neanderthal or mated with them and created these early humans that thought out a way to fight back against these adversarial vicious human variants known as the Neanderthal.

I also have a problem with his theory that the population of humans on earth was wiped out by the Neanderthal predation, until there were only 50 human individuals left where he illustrates how these 50 survivors who were the prey of these Neanderthal that salvaged humankind from annihilation by transforming into aggressive and predatory beings that fought back --- and spreading across the globe, killing (and sometimes eating) all Neanderthals in their path, as well as Neanderthal looking Hominids, until the Neanderthal themselves became extinct --- I have a problem with this theory since it sounds like something right out of a movie script and not reality in the sight of Genuine Archaeologists and Historical experts. Although I myself do not dispute it since we have been left to our own devices of flawed historical facts that has left us all alone to rely on the possible inaccuracy of Carbon Dating and the periods of millennial passages of time. That went by concealing the artifacts of evidence left behind and also concealing the archaeological residue of these artifacts.

 Furthermore, Vendramini describes this global migration through Europe, Africa, Asia and Australia and the Americas, as a 20,000-kilometer blitzkrieg. It did not end until these hyper-aggressive humans -- our ancestors the Cro Magnons -- were the only hominids left alive. It was the first instance of evolution by genocide he says. One of these first ever Genocides taught the lessons of how to organize and execute an invasion to overcome the enemy ---- if this genocide of a blitzkrieg actually took place to kill off the Neanderthal where they eventually became extinct.

Not only have we had the wrong impression of the nature and behaviour of Neanderthals, argues Ventramini, "But we have been fed sentimental, anthropomorphic visuals of them as well. Neanderthal," he says, were primates and would have looked like primates although some them may have been of a different variant of the Homo Sapiens. Some of them were not supposed to be considered clean-shaven with protruding noses and curly hair much like a Homo Sapiens would have. These guys, he says expounds, or clearly explains with elaborate detail that they "came from the frozen north -- they had flat, ape- like noses, large nocturnal eyes, and were covered in thick hair and were six times stronger than the average human. They were not a pretty sight."

Leading authority on Neanderthals, Professor John Shea of Stony Brook

University in New York, is enthusiastic about Neanderthal predation theory: Danny Ventramini presents a truly unique and innovative picture of the role of Neanderthal predation in human evolution. He pulls together countless different threads of scientific evidence to re-cast Neanderthals as apex predators, proverbial wolves with knives who were effective rivals with our ancestors.

"His thesis," continues Shea, that many physical, social, and psychological characteristics now seen as uniquely human are direct results of The Neanderthal predation on our ancestors will be sure to ignite controversy in scientific meetings, university classrooms, and among any group of people genuinely interested in human origin or possible evolution of humanity or the Homo Sapiens which was created literally by God with a soul according to Genesis 2: 7.

Neanderthals did not have souls since they were created as a beast before the time of Adam and Eve dating back hundreds of thousands of years to the time of the existence of dinosaurs. Where Adam and Eve were also at a later period created perhaps before or after dinosaurs became extinct or alongside dinosaurs that were already living at the time. Because of the passages of many many centuries that have gone by, like hundreds of thousands of years since the creation of Adam and Eve, this hypothesis of disproving of proving that Adam and Eve was either created before or after dinosaurs; or co-existed and being created during and alongside with dinosaurs that were already existing at the time or not; leaves us all in the dark.

 Regardless of what ever evidence that may have existed whether through historical cultural records of written languages left behind and every engravened symbols of these writings on the interior walls of caves or archaeological evidence alone that appears on historical excavation sites around the world. Here the only hint we have is that it is possible that either dinosaurs were created before Adam and Eve or that these beasts known as dinosaurs existed and were alive at the time of the creation of Adam and

Eve. Where this hint could be found in the Authorized King James Version Bible that cattle were part of this creation alongside dinosaurs and that the term "beast" could refer also to dinosaurs that was part of this very early creation according to Genesis 1: 24.

Also it may be possible that the serpent in the Garden of Eden may have infected Adam and Eve with sin by temptation --- causing their descendants to possibly mingle with the Neanderthal and perhaps were sexually active with the Neanderthal who were beasts without a soul, who had the potential for violence and rape crimes, and further inspiring Cain to commit murder. Where chaos and violence infiltrated and spread out throughout the whole earth where God was not pleased at all with man here according to Genesis 6: 5, 6, 7. Here the Neanderthal may have been a variant specie of Homo Sapiens. Who knows what type of species of humanity or different entities of humans existed in the time before or at postlapsarian time following the creation and existence of Adam and Eve and the visitation of the Sons of God, on and to this planet.

CHAPTER 2
LOUCHE KINGS AND QUEENS

The term "Louche" refers to a person or authority that is involved in scandal or is not considered a reputable or decent person. Here Kings and Queens have the power of privilege and that advantage of having the power through monetary means to offer bribes in exchange from keeping those who have witnessed to testify in a court of law for an unlawful act of financial deception or fraud. That is committed against financial investors by these Kings or Queens of Authority. Here these types of allegations bring on the sins of adultery and fornication and infidelity in the one who is a king or Queen because of the deception that has been committed by these possible allegations in order to retaliate in retribution. Here this type of retribution may bring on conflict between the parties involved or even murder. One example was England's "King John I" who reigned from 1199 to 1216 nicknamed " Bad King John." Here "King John I" acquired a villainous image that has been reproduced time and time again in popular culture, including film adaptations of Robin Hood and a play by Shakespeare. Here "King John I" had inherited a kingdom that have had been at ongoing holy wars previously by his brother "King Richard I" in which the treasury or coffers were emptied due to these ongoing wars. Here through the greed of "King John I" he went ahead and raised taxes that would have been wildly unpopular. Then "King John I" had also had gained a reputation for treachery prior to becoming king. Then in 1192, he attempted to seize "King Richard's I" throne while he was held captive in Austria. "King John I" even tried to negotiate extending his brother's imprisonment and he was lucky to be pardoned by his brother "King Richard I" after his release.

What further damned "King John I" in his contemporaries' eyes was his lack of piety. Because for medieval England, a good king was a pious one and "King John I" had numerous affairs with married noblewomen which was considered deeply immoral. Medieval kings were also meant to be brave. Also "King John I" was nicknamed "Softsword" for losing English land in France including the powerful Duchy of Normandy. When France invaded in 1216, "King John I " was almost 3 leagues away or about 15 miles away by the time any of his men realized he had abandoned them.

Finally, while "King John I" was in part responsible for the creation of the Magna Carta, a document widely regarded as the foundation of English justice. His participation was at best unwilling. Here in this type of mindset that "King John I" had; is that, it is easy to see how the Ancient Blood of Violence in the justice system would evolve and become corrupt with the justice in the court of law where there was regards in the sentences and convictions and inappropriate punishments in these sentences and convictions coming from a Court or Judge. Here this lack of appropriate justice carried on in these ancient periods of centuries gone by and so like it was back then, so does it carry on now. Like for example the many wars that have plagued humanity down the centuries, not only mentioned many times in the Authorized King James Version Bible; but what has been reported by humanity in the past or recent 100 hundred years or so to the present now, not only in the media and online but also revealed on social media. When here in these ancient periods going back to May 1215, a group of barons marched an army south, forcing "King John I" to renegotiate England's governance, and ultimately neither side upheld their end of the bargain and so it goes that in the end that nothing is accomplished to govern a form of legislative justice of good understanding that is favourable in order to avoid this transgression of Ancient Blood of Violence according to Proverbs 13: 15.

Another example here of Ancient Blood of Violence is the threat of civil war. King Edward II who reigned from 1307-1327, that even before he was even king, Edward II made the Medieval royal error unapologetically surrounding himself with favourites: this meant that throughout his reign, the threat of civil war was ever-present. Peirs Gaveston was King Edward's II most notable favourite, so much so that contemporaries described them as: "two kings in one kingdom, one in name and the other in deed." Which would suggest that in deed may have meant that homosexuality was part of this friendship they may have had and that it explains why Piers Gaveston was King Edward's II notable favourite being lovers where their relationship enraged the barons who felt slighted by Gaveston's position.

Edward was forced to exile his friend and institute the Ordinances of 1311, that were the restriction of royal powers for whatever restrictions and reasons that were ordained at that period in history. Yet at the last minute perhaps by temptation, he disregarded the Ordinances of this restriction, and brought back Gaveston who was swiftly executed by the barons.

Further damaging his popularity, King Edwards II was determined to pacify or to please or ease their burden toward the Scots who having followed his father on his earlier northern campaigns. In June 1314, King Edward II marched one of medieval England's mightiest armies to Scotland but was crushed by Robert the Bruce at the Battle of Bannockburn. This humiliating defeat was followed by widespread harvest failures and famine. Although it was not King Edwards II 's fault, the king exacerbated or with being very bitter discontentment by continuing to make his closest friends very rich; and in 1321 civil war broke out. King Edward II had also alienated his allies. His wife Isabella (daughter of a French king) then left to France to sign a treaty. Instead she plotted against King Edward II with Roger Morimer, 1st Earl of March, and together they invaded England with a small army. A year later in 1327, King Edward II was captured and was forced to abdicate or resign as the ruling king of England. Here it is a real burden for kings too rule knowing that they too can be held accountable as well or fall to a former ally or an on-going enemy according to Proverbs 24: 6, 7, 8, 9, 10.

King Richard II that reigned from 1377 to 1399 was a son of the Black Prince Edward III, here also Richard II became king at age 10. So, a series of regency councils have also governed the country of England by King Richard II side because of his young age of ten as the King of England. Here King Richard II who was another king with a poor Shakespearean reputation having the Ancient Blood of Violence in his character as well as those characters of the regency council members in authority in office had character's together that were so bad that King Richard II who was only 14 years old along with this regency council that ran his government here was that his government brutally suppressed the Peasant's Revolt of 1381. But it is possible that according to some, this act of aggression may have been against teenage King Richard's II wishes. Along with a volatile court full of powerful men wrestling for influence for the greed that they had and negligence of governing and debating with those men who do not want to cause any confrontation in war ---- this governing body of unjust powerful men in this volatile court of debate were in numbers being the God of this world according to 2nd Corinthians 4: 4 or of their world going back in that ancient time or period in history where they were out numbering those who uphold the justice of God that have left King Richard II with inheriting the Hundred Year War with France. The Hundred Year War was a territorial conflict fought between England and France in the late Middle ages. It was waged between 1337 to 1453. So, the title " Hundred Year War " isn't quite accurate: the war actually lasted 116 years. A real prime example of the Ancient Blood of Violence that brought man to a Neanderthal mindset level so low that not even the Neanderthal had a conflict among their tribes that lasted as long as 116 years.

The basis of the drawn-out series of wars originated from disputed claims to the French throne from the royal families of England's House of Plantagenet and its rival, the French royal House of Valois. Here not only is this conflict of this war brutal because of how long it lasted but here this Ancient Blood of Violence has even originated within humanity's own kind. Where they have enemies in their own households? According to Matthew 10: 35, 36, 37, 38? Was this war waged by Religious debate and conflicts between infidels of the Bible and those who were Christians? This shows how brutal Religious persecution can be and how this Ancient Blood of Violence was so common that billions of years down the history of Planet earth and the many millennial years of existence of earth has brought us all the way back to the time of Adam and Eve with the beginning of these sins of the Ancient Blood of violence ever since the first murder of Abel by Cain in the time of Genesis. Which was also a murder that was because God who showed Abel favor for his sacrifice while Cain being envious of Abel's true and common sense of faith toward God led Cain to murder Abel in Cold blood because of his jealousy and envy. And that the family of Adam and Eve may have been dysfunctional after Eve had sinned with committing the first sin of the human race with that serpent in the Garden of Eden. (I go into detail on this topic of Adam and Eve in my books "Pyromancy" "Open Tomb, Aviation 666, Monsters of Genesis" and "Magistrates of Damnation")

 Here the effects of this Hundred Year War, which involved 5 generations of kings, not only brought about innovations in military weaponry but also created stronger national identities for both France with their distinctive languages and cultures involving the religious concept involving the acceptance of Biblical Doctrine. Although they had other more conforming adherence to the more many different Biblically corrupt translations of the true Authorized King James Version Bible, where here after these 5 kings of generations passed away; the Hundred Year War ended. But because after this conflict in our world continued in conflict the corrupt faith that the general population in the world had, it was passed down from every sovereign king in his generation to the next sovereign king of his generation and so on. Bringing us here to the rulers of today that have a corrupt justice system according to Psalms 82 : 1, 2, 3, 4 and Ecclesiastes 5: 8, 9. Also the ways of governing a peaceful and sovereign nation that has rejected the critical morals of God where peaceful governing here requires us to accept the morals of God as it is mentioned here in this scripture according to Psalms 72 : 1, 2, 3, 4, 5, 6, 7, 8, 9.

So here the Hundred Year War that was expensive and with the volatile court full of powerful men wrestling for influence, King Richard II inherited this Hundred Year War. England was already heavily taxed. The poll tax of 1381 was the final straw. In Kent and Essex, resentful peasants rose up against landowners in protest.

Going Back to June 1377, having outlived his son and heir, Edward of Woodstock. By the practices of medieval kingship, the crown thus was passed to Edward of Woodstock's son --- then 10-year-old Richard --- who became King Richard II. Richard's reign was beset by problems of ruling in a minority at a time of great social upheaval --- particularly caused by economic pressures of the Black Death. King Richard II was also a capricious king who made powerful enemies, and his appetite for revenge ended with being deposed by his cousin Henry Bolingbroke --- who became Henry IV. However, King Henry's IV usurpation or take possession without rights made the line of kingship more complex, with the Plantagenet family now in competing cadet branches of "Lancaster" (descendant of John Gaunt) and "York" (descendant from Edmund, Duke of York as well as Lionel, Duke of Clarence). This complicated backdrop set the stage for dynastic conflict and confusion and a cause open for civil war amongst the English nobility in the mid-15th century. Here are the 3 Lancastrian 3 Yorkist kings in order: Henry IV -- Henry V --- Henry -- VI ---- Edward IV --- Edward V --- Richard III.

Aged 14 at the time King Richard II faced the peasant rebels when they arrived in London and it may have not been just the peasants where this rebellion may have taken place but those affected by this heavily taxed condition where the tax poll became the final straw. Here King Richard II instead of arresting them since there may have been many of these protesters who were causing this violence. King Richard II may have allowed them to return home after the violence subsided. However, further upheaval in the following weeks after this tax polling saw the rebel leaders executed.

This suppression of the revolt during King Richard's II reign fed his belief in his divine right as king. This absolutism eventually brought King Richard's II to blows with parliament and the Lords Appellant, a group of 5 powerful nobles including his own uncle , Thomas Wookstock who opposed King Richard II and his influential adviser, Michael de la Pole, that when King Richard II finally came of age he sought retribution for his counselors' earlier betrayals, manifesting in a series of dramatic executions as he purged the Lords Apellant, including his uncle who was accused of treason and executed. He also Sent John of Gaunt's son (King Richard's Cousin) Henry Bolingbroke into exile. Unfortunately for King Richard II, Henry returned to England to overthrow him in 1399 and with popular support for Henry Bolingbroke he was crowned King Henry IV.

Here King Richard II fell to tyranny through the 1390's, his exiled cousin Henry of Bolingbroke eldest surviving son of John of Gaunt duke of Lancaster, returned to England to claim the throne. The childless King Richard II was forced to Abdicate and Lancastrian rule began on September 30 / 1399. Although King Henry IV invaded England in June 1399 with a small force that quickly grew in numbers. Meeting little resistance, he deposed of King Richard II and had himself crowned king. King Richard II was thought to have been starved to death in captivity, although questions remain in regards to his final fate. Here this is a Lancastrian rule was the multiple kings appointed in a certain order like King Henry IV and King Henry V and King Henry VI and King Edward IV and King Edward V and King Richard III, meant to bring perhaps tyranny to an end. But as the Bible calls it? It is all confusion in the name of the Babylonian Life style of the life of society , community and rule by Magistrates and Kings on this planet by Royalty and Royal family dynasties which could be considered secular and Babylonian in nature like for instance the War of the Roses that were a series of bloody civil wars for the Throne of England between two competing Royal Families : The House of York and the House of Lancaster. Both members of the Old Royal Plantagenet Family. They waged war between 1455 and 1485, the War of the Roses earned its flowery name because the white rose was the badge of the Yorks, and the Red Rose was the badge of the Lancastrians. After 30 years of political manipulation, horrific carnage and brief periods of peace, the wars ended and a new Royal Dynasty emerged and leading other of these dynasties to suffer the same fate as the infection known as the Babylonian temptation of Lust of sex and food, and materialism , and Greed and Power that has led to confusion and becoming confounded through war and peace down the centuries according to the Strong's Exhaustive Concordance of the Bible of the Old Testament # 894 from # 1101 which refers to "confusion; Babel (i.e. Babylon), including Babylonia and the Babylonian Empire : "to overflow" (especially with oil); by implementing to mix also (demonimation from 1098) to fodder : anoint , confound, x fade, mingle, mix (self) , give provender, temper."

Now this confusion and immoral activity of the Babylonian life style steers to the queens of history. Here we have Marie Antoinette who was the queen of France from 1744 through 1792. In fact, she was the last queen before the French revolution. This queen was obsessed with the Babylonian Life style of sex and food and most of all material things she had a penchant for which was expensive things that turned many of the commoners against her for her love of opulence and glamour. For instance, a Young woman called the countess de La Mott entered the French court in 1785, and pretended to be a close friend of Antionette's. She was able to con a member of high society into believing the royal was in love with him. So she hired a prostitute to pretend to be Antionette, and seduced him and convinced the man of high society that Antionette was interested in purchasing a giant diamond necklace for $1,600,000 livres (approximately $ 12,000,000 today). Of course, this money was never paid, because the queen herself Marie Antoinette had no knowledge of this conspiracy against her and also the jewelers were almost bankrupt. Even though she was eventually proven innocent in court, the public still was swayed against Marie Antoinette. The queen was all but despised when she was executed at the end of her reign. An unfortunate end to a queen who loved the secular life style of the elite of the wealthy and perhaps even the famous of their time.

Irene of Athens ruled Byzantine in some capacity from 780 to 802 A.D. But her biggest power grab came after her son, Constantine VI, had overthrown her and attempted to gain power for himself. Eventually, the two reconciled and co-ruled together, but that wasn't enough for Irene. So, in 786, Constantine turned public opinion against him when he divorced his wife to marry his mistress, and Irene took advantage of the situation by conspiring with the help of others against her son. She had her supporters arrest her son and blind Constantine by gouging his eyes out. By most accounts, he died soon after this was done, though some speculate he and his wife Theodore lived a private life in exile.

Marguerite of Valois was exiled from court and publicly opposed her husband which was unheard of at the time. Marguerite was the queen of France and Navarre (parts of present-day Spain and France) from 1572 to 1599. She had a difficult relationship with her husband, brother, and mother, forcing her to think outside the box in order to survive her ordeal of immorality. When the Queen was unable to provide her husband (the king) with an heir, she was sent to live with her brother, Henry III. A scandal followed her. It was rumored that during her time away from her husband, she became pregnant with her lover's son due to craving and wanting sexual and perverted satisfaction according to Proverbs 13: 25. This infuriated her brother and led to her exile from both his castle and her husband's castle as well according to Proverbs 18: 19. Marguerite eventually was able to convince her husband to let her come home to realize that their marriage would never be the same again. This led her to do something unheard of, she abandoned her husband and her family. And fled to an entirely new area, and appealed to the Holy Catholic League as a leader in her own right. What was more scandalous? Her husband was a Protestant, and the two factions of Christianity had been at odds at one another and in conflict. Where the birth of the uncertainty in the truth of Christianity developed. Here they both had professed that the one against the other knows God better where both these two factions emerged into apostasy according to Titus 1: 16.

Catherine Howard, the fifth wife of Henry VIII, was executed for committing adultery. Catherine Howard was the queen of England for 18 months, from July 1540 to November 1541. She became the fifth wife of King Henry VIII when she was still a teenager, while the king was nearing 50. Their marriage was happy, by all accounts, until it was revealed that Catherine Howard had committed adultery and had relationships with three men: Thomas Culpeper, Henry Mannock, and Francis Dereham. What was even worse was that she made Dereham her secretary, and it was believed by many that she also cheated on the king with both Dereham and Culpeper.

Eventually Catherine Howard was caught in these adulterous affairs with both these men, Francis Dereham and Thomas Culpeper. Although Catherine denied vehemently these relationships and affairs with both these men. But both men admitted to these affairs after being tortured. They eventually were tried and found guilty. Through the Ancient Blood of Violence Francis Dereham was hanged, and drawn and quartered or that is tied to a horse and dragged to the hangman, hanged, then tied to four horses spurred to run in different directions. While Thomas Culpeper was beheaded. Catherine Howard on the other hand, was never put on trial and was directly sentenced to death. She was beheaded in 1542. Here the future Anti-Christ or Beast known as a tyrannical One World Leader would take the same approach of directly beheading citizens without a trial for refusing to swear allegiance to his One World Government according to Revelation 20: 4.

Queen Caroline Matilda and her lover essentially controlled the entire Danish government by themselves, until they were overthrown. The affair of Danish queen Caroline Matilda and Johann Friedrich Struensee is one of the biggest scandals in Danish history because it is widely believed that the princess, Louise Augusta, was their illegitimate daughter. Here Princess Louise Augusta married Frederik Christian of Augustenborg in 1786. Together they had a daughter, Caroline Amalie, Queen of Christian 8.
 Louise Augusta was officially the Daughter of Christian 7 and Queen Caroline Matilda, but it is almost certain that the king's physician, Johann Friedrich Struensee was her real father. Louise Augusta divorced both of her biological parents early after the revelation of their relationship. Caroline Matilda was exiled, and Johann Friedrich Struensee was executed the year after Louise Augusta's daughter was born. After the politically arranged marriage to Duke Frederik Christian of Augustenborg, the couple lived for a long time at Christanborg, where Louise Augusta was often the center or the court or governing power in politics. Throughout her life, she had a close relationship with her brother Frederik 6, whom she also

supported after he and her spouse had come into political conflict. These types of conflicts always bring on domestic violence and, in some cases, even political upheaval in most cases resulting in the Ancient Blood of Violence according to Proverbs 17: 1. It was clear to everyone in Danish high society and that the court of King Christian VII was mentally unstable. He was said to have been "psychologically unstable and suffered from anxiety attacks, outbursts of anger, paranoia, self-mutilation and hallucinations," according to the Copenhagen Post. Enter Johann Friedrich Struensee, a doctor who became a close confidante of the king. Quickly Johann Friedrich Struensee and the Queen, who shared similar political views, began an affair and convinced the king to give absolute power to Johann Friedrich Struensee. For 10 months, Denmark was ruled by queen Caroline Matilda and this German doctor Johann Friedrich Struensee and the two significantly changed Denmark's political landscape. Here the king was ultimately convinced by their enemies that the two lovers were conspiring to kill him, and had Johann Friedrich Struensee murdered and exiled Caroline Matilda.

Mary, Queen of Scotland, is believed to have orchestrated the death of her second husband, Henry Stewart. aka Lord Darnley. Mary, the queen of Scotland from 1542 to 1567, had a lifelong feud with Queen Elizabeth I, her cousin, but history has since regarded her as a tragic figure in that conflict. Potentially murdering her husband, however, remains a bona-fide scandal. Mary married her cousin, the Lord Darnley, after her first husband died of an ear infection. "As soon as he gets married to her, he started to try to undermine her," "Mary Queen Of Scotland," director Josie Rourke told people. Here it is suggested by director Josie Rourke that Henry Stuart, Lord Darnley Queen Mary Stuart's husband had a gay affair in bed with Queen Mary Stuart's gay male courtesan or prostitute David Rizzio on her wedding night catching them in bed as she walked in on them while they were in bed on her wedding night of 1565. Henry Stuart, Lord Darnley and David Rizzio having a sexual relationship is definitely true to history historian John Guy tells PEOPLE Magazine. Here Lord Darnley is believed to have orchestrated to kill David Rizzio, a close friend of Queen Mary of Scotland right in front of her while she was pregnant. Soon after, Lord Darnley was murdered. Historians don't totally agree on how he died some say he died in an explosion, while others say he was strangled. But they all confirm that the Scottish people were suspicious of Queen Mary, especially since she quickly married the prime suspect in his murder, the Earl of Bothwell. The growing discontentments and suspicions about Queen Mary, forced her to abdicate the throne and flee to England, where she was eventually executed in 1587 for plotting to kill Queen Elizabeth I whom she was known to have a feud with. Here Queen Mary Stuart and Queen Elizabeth neither considered to be a villain but instead it was suggested that they were two smart women in power who were trying to do the right thing for their people. But both women especially Mary consistently fail because of the men who were threatened by their gender that may have caused friction between Queen Mary Stuart and Queen Elizabeth I in their relationship.

Catherine the Great Organized a coup to overthrow her husband. Russian queen Catherine the Great was neither Russian nor really named Catherine, is remembered as one of Russia's greatest leaders. But it wasn't always smooth sailing. Catherine came into power when her mother-in-law died in 1762, and her husband Peter became emperor. However, he quickly became unpopular with the people when he ended the war with Prussia and made no secret for his distaste of Russia. Catherine, seeing the growing discontentment among the people, quickly made plans to over throw her husband. Peter abdicated but was assassinated eight days later. While there was no evidence directly tying Catherine to his death, it was committed by her supporters, and public opinion that held her responsible for her husband's assassination.

Isabella of France was known by some as the She-Wolf of France. Queen Isabella ruled England from 1308 to 1327, first alongside her husband King Edward II. One of the most notorious women in English history Isabella of France led an invasion of England that ultimately resulted in the disposition of her king and husband Edward II who she was unhappily married to. Then through the invasion and rebellion of England in January 1327 had her husband imprisoned and ultimately executed and so she became known as the She-Wolf of France and then continued to rule as a regent of England with her new lover whom she had an affair with who was Roger Mortimer. Isabella may have possibly after getting involved in this affair with Roger Mortimer may have agreed at this point with Roger Mortimer to dispose King Edward II and oust the Despenser family. Queen Isabella was increasingly neglected by her husband, who was infatuated with numerous men over the course of their relationship who King Edward II may have also been infatuated with Hugh le Despenser. So, this may have been the reason for her Ancient Blood of Violence against her husband King Edward II and his imprisonment and execution and ousting the Despenser family. Also, Hugh le Despenser was for a time a chief Advisor to King Edward II. Also referred to as the "Elder Despenser" who was created a baron in 1925 and Earl of Winchester in 1322.

King Henry VII's love for Anne Boleyn caused the English to break away from the Roman Catholic Church and create their own Church. King Henry VII's love for Anne Boleyn is the reason that the Church of England exists in Catholicism. Divorce was strictly prohibited by the Authorized King James Version Bible and perhaps the Church of England which may have been at the time a form of true worship towards Christ which became corrupted by these doctrines of infidelity brought on by the corrupt and adulterous ways of King Henry VII. So, the English broke away from the Roman Catholic Church which was considered an Apostate Church of Christ according to Revelation 17: 1, 2, 3, 4, 5, 6, 7. So when King Henry VII fell out of love with his wife Catherine and in Love with Anne Boleyn, their marriage had to end. So, Anne Boleyn and King Henry VII got married in 1533, and ruled together until 1536, when King Henry VII order her execution on charges of infidelity and incest. In 1536 England's King Henry VII accused his second wife Anne Boleyn, who had been crowned queen in 1533, of charges including adultery and incest and conspiracy against the king. In actuality, the king grew bored of her, and agitated by her inability to provide him with a male heir. And so at her trial, she was found guilty, and on May 19, 1936 she was taken to Tower Green in London, where she was beheaded by a French swordsman, rather than the standard axe- wielding executioner. The reason for this? Perhaps to inflict more harm and suffering on Ann Boleyn during the execution causing a great and messy and mutilated killing or execution of Anne Boleyn as means of retribution coming from King Henry VII's Ancient Blood of Violence. Historians believe the charges against her were perhaps false and that were issued by King Henry VII to remove Anne Boleyn as his wife and enable him to marry his third wife, Jane Seymour in hopes of producing a male heir which Anne Boleyn was not able or not willing to provide for King Henry VII.

The following is eight sex addicted Monarchs in history starting with one the most notorious who was Caligula Emperor of Rome, 37 - 41 A.D. In our history we read mostly about civil wars, historical events, discoveries, and inventions. But we rarely learn about the sex lives and sexual preferences of people who ruled over our ancient forefathers. Here Caligula Emperor of Rome is a well-known and enduring sensualist. Caligula was known to seduce the wives of his Senators right in front of them. He used to bring home prostitutes and engage in affairs with story-telling performing female dancers who express sexual body movements or who are also known as pantomime performers. In addition to marrying four women, he used to sleep with his sisters as well as he was saying in a seductive remark quote "c'mon." Caligula was a violent and insane person and it is hard to believe that after just five years on the throne his own guards through the Ancient Blood of Violence killed him.

Henry I --- King of England, 1100 - 1135. King Henry I of England held the record of having the most illegitimate children. He fathered more than twenty illegitimate kids. According to the "New York Times" he is the "Undisputed royal record holder for fathering illegitimate children." Henry had two wives Matilda of Scotland, and Adeliza of Louvain. He had two children with Matilda and none with Adeliza. But that's not it, thanks to his countless affairs with some very fertile women, he had a huge lineage of illegitimate children. He whored around all the time, from his teens until his death, sex was the only game he liked and craved. Born in 1068 and died December 1st 1135 at age 66- 67. Apparently, Henry I of England died in 1135 at age 66-67 allegedly from eating too many lampreys (a fish). According to the Authorized King James Version Bible eating excessively can be considered sowing to the flesh where you reap corruption and death. Also eating excessively is also considered gluttony or a sin and when lust has been conceived it brings forth sin and sin when it is finished with you, it brings forth death. According James 1: 15 and Galatians 6: 8 and Proverbs 23: 19, 20, 21. It is also interesting to note that the Apostate Roman Catholic Church commemorates the crucifixion of Christ by not eating meat on Friday but in its place the Church has ordained the commemoration of eating fish only on Friday excluding all other forms of meats like beef or ham etc. Here this commemoration is the worship of Christ and his virgin mother Mary as an idol being and becoming a sacrifice, or eating or sacrificing this fish and being a sacrifice or partakers of the cross or altar and dying in the end because of eating this fish excessively being in the flesh who are not born again by blood and water in order to receive the

Holy Spirit. Also those who are born again by blood and water in order to receive the Holy Spirit are prohibited to eat fish (I go into detail about this topic of eating fish as ordained as a commemoration by the Roman Catholic Church in my first book "Pyromancy "), if they eat even a very small amount of fish they can die according to Romans 14: 23 and 1st Corinthians 10: 18, 19, 20, 21, 22.

Marie of Romania --- Queen of Romania, 1914 - 1927 --- Queen Marie of Romania 's husband Ferdinand I was the King of Romania and was in charge of the kingdom Marie was running the affairs of the state. Queen Marie was a strong popular figure in the world. Also, just like other popular figures of that time Queen Marie wasn't a fan of Monogamy either. Out of many men she had, Prince Barbu Stirbey was her favorite. Many Historians believe that Prince Barbu Stirbey was the real father of Mircea, her youngest son. Apart from that, Marie is said to have had affairs with her newspaperman Waldorf Astor, Lieutenant Zizi Cantacuzene and Canadian adventurer Joe Boyle. It is obvious that she didn't just have one type.

Henry VIII -- King of England, 1509 - 1547, Henry the most known and popular of Kings when it came to being a womanizer of many women. Step one --- Get a wife -- Step two --- Take her out by murder when she can't produce a male heir ----Step three Get a sidepiece like another woman ---- Step four ---- Get rid of the wife through a divorce or by getting her killed ---- Step five ------ Marry a mistress ---- Step six ----- Start from step one again.

Apart from having six wives, Henry VIII used to have prostitutes over all the time. He even slept with Mary Boleyn, his second wife's sister. It is said that he fathered two of her kids too. Also, Historian Kelly Hart believes that Henry VIII had at least 12 mistresses outside his wives.

Henry IV and Margaret of France --- King and Queen of France, 1589 -- 1599. Neither Henry nor Margaret had a decent relationship with the whole fidelity issue during their marriage. "The Green Gallant" was Henry IV 's nickname because of his popularity among the ladies. He was known to leave his armies to shack up with one of his many mistresses. During the sex he had with all these mistresses he had contracted gonorrhea that nearly wiped him out. In order to marry Marie de Medici of the famous and wealthy Florentine family, he annulled his childless marriage to Margaret. But Margaret was no angel either. Out of her many affairs, the most famous one was with Joseph Boniface de Mole, who later was tortured and executed for plotting against the King. The Encyclopedia states that she was known for her licentiousness or lack of moral ways or lack of sexual restraint.

Louis XIV -- King of France, 1638 - 1715 --- The Sun King, like Gretchen Weiners, Louis XIV King of France had beautiful hair that was full of secrets or possibly having dirty Skeletons in his closet. With Catherine - Henriette Bellier, who essentially taught Louis XIV about the Quote: "business cycle" (if you know what I mean) or about possibly teaching him sexual acts and how to encounter women for sex when he was a teen. He began as a teen after possibly being taught these things by Catherine Henriette Bellier to begin his conquest to becoming king and his possible reason for his rise to the throne. Then after when he was married to Queen Marie- Therese with whom he had six children with, he then had four other children with this impressively - named lady, and also had a daughter with Claude de Vin des Eillets, and then after this he also had seven kids with Marquise de Montespan. And this was just the baby mothers! He had many other affairs; and as well as a secret wife in Madame de Maintenon.

King Edward VII -- King of England, 1901 - 1910 --- King Edward VII had a lot of nicknames that truly reflected his personality. He was called "Bertie," which was a short version of his first name Albert. He was called "Tum Tum" because of his fat tummy. However, he was most commonly known as "Edward the Caresser" and "Dirty Bertie", because of the multiple mistresses and numerous sexual relationships that he had. His mistresses included Winston Churchill's mother; the beautiful Jennie Jerome also known as Lady Randolph Churchill. Surprisingly he had another mistress called Alice Keppel, who was the great Grandmother of Camilla Parker Bowles, the wife of the current Prince of Wales, Charles.

King Edward VII had a special sex toy called the "sex chair" which he used while having sex. It is said that King Edward VII lost his virginity when he was 19, and since then he had sex with at least four women every week until his death fifty years later. Historians did the math and they believe that he could possibly have slept with between 15, 000 and 18,000 women during his lifetime. The image of the skull on the cover of this book with the dagger going through it; is a symbolic message of violence with a weapon and that it is also a symbolic message of the dagger going through the brain representing the evil of the spiritual character of mankind's sins of adultery and fornication and excessive lust and murder. Where the dagger going through the skull and brain represents the harm humanity is doing to itself by all these different sins of lust and hatred and violence. Turning the soul and spirit into a depraved and despicable state of corruption that inflicts harm to humanity by violence and murder /or physical corruption of the flesh by these sins of hatred and violence and lust that leads to death eventually. Since the brain in the skull is the partial workings of the soul and spirit according to Galatians 5: 16, 17, 18, 19, 20, 21.

Here also is the treacherous and torturous abuse of a prisoner by Fidel Castro who this prisoner by the name of Jean-Paul Sarte helped rouse the conscience of France by writing an introduction to the Question by Henri Alleg, a small book that recounted the torture of a french opponent of the Algerian war in Algerian prisons. One had to decide, Sarte wrote, "whether to be the torturer or the tortured. Alleg suffered the fate of all those tortured, Sarte wrote, and he showed" the calm courage of the victim," as well as a modesty and lucidity (or a presumed capacity to perceive the truth directly and instantaneously.) which wakes us and show us the truth.

Now Armando Valladares, a Cuban poet, awakes us to the same task and truths. How ironic that a year after Sarte wrote these words, he visited Cuba and proclaimed to the world that Fidel Castro was motivated above all by a hatred for the word " injustice " used against those who commit perverted judgment and justice, and that he had brought about the liberation of Cuba from despotism or absolute tyrannical power. It has taken us 25 years to find out the terrible reality --- Mr. Castro has created a new despotism that has institutionalized torture as a mechanism of social control.

At the beginning of his book, the author of "Against All Hope: The prison Memoirs of Armando Valladares" was a young employee of Postal Savings Bank of Cuba's New revolutionary government. His misfortune was to be a man with outspoken opinions according to Proverbs 15: 7. He openly expressed his philosophical opposition to the communist system and as a result his home was searched by the agents of the political police. They found nothing, but he was arrested as the counterrevolutionary and spent a nightmare of 22 years in Mr. Castro's prisons. In his introduction, Mr. Valladares speculates that when the truth about Cuba's political prisoners is made known, mankind will feel the revulsion it felt when the crimes of Stalin were brought to light. "It is not too tough a judgment."

How did a revolution whose leader promised a humanist, non- communist and democratic revolution descend to such depravity? In his memoir of the revolutionary struggle, "Family Portrait With Fidel" (1984), Carlos Franqui, the editor of the official revolutionary newspaper, "Revolucion," for some years after the Cuban Revolution, notes how shocked he was to hear reports of the torture of counterrevolutionary suspects. Bringing news of this to Mr. Castro, Mr. Franqui quickly learned that the torture had the leader's blessings. Mr. Franqui points out that the decision to execute the former Cuban president Fulgencio Batista's worst goons created "a new repressive power that would be implacable." When Mr. Franqui raised the issue of the moral degradation torture implies, Mr. Castro told him that it annihilates the enemy and hence was necessary.

Until this publication of this book, "Against All Hope" in a serviceable translation by Andrew Hurley, we had not had a full picture of the brutality meted out or measured out to real and imaginary opponents by the Castro dictatorship. What Mr. Valladares gives us is a picture of the hell that was the Cuba he lived in, and the story of how one man's deep Christian faith enabled him to sustain the most evil treatment and never abandon hope, no matter how fruitless hope appeared according to Romans 8: 24, 25.

Mr. Valladares and other prisoners who refused "political rehabilitation" were forced to live in the greatest heat and the dampest cold without clothes. They were regularly beaten, shot at and sometimes killed; they were thrown into punishment cells, including the dreaded "drawer cells," specially constructed units that make South Vietnam's infamous tiger cages seem like honey quarters. Eventually together with several others, Mr. Valladares plotted an escape from their prison on the Isle of Pines. But the boat that was to pick them up never arrived. He and his accomplices were brought back to their cells and given no medical attention, though Mr. Valladares had fractured three bones in his foot during the escape attempt.

The retribution was swift. Mr. Valladares writes: "Guards returned us to the cells and stripped us again. They didn't close the cell door, and that detail caught my attention. I was sitting on the floor; outside I heard the voices of several approaching soldiers... They were going to settle accounts with us, collect what we owed them for having tried to escape... They were armed with thick twisted electric cables and truncheons or clubs... Suddenly everything was whirl--- my head spun around in terrible vertigo. They beat me as I lay on the floor. One of them pulled at my arm to turn me over and expose my back so he could beat me more easily. And the cables fell more directly on me. The beating felt as if they were branding me with a red-hot branding iron, but then suddenly I experienced the most intense, unbearable and brutal pain of my life. One of the guards had jumped with all his weight on my broken throbbing leg."

That treatment was typical. In the punishment cells, prisoners were kept in total darkness. Guards dumped buckets of urine and feces over the prisoners who ward off rats and roaches as they tried to sleep. Fungus grew on Mr. Valladares because he was not allowed to wash off the filth. Sleep was impossible. Guards constantly awoke the men with long poles to insure they got no rest. Illness and disease were a constant. Even at the end, when the authorities were approving his release, Mr. Valadares was held in solitary confinement in a barren room with fluorescent lights turned on 24 hours a day. By then he was partially paralyzed through malnutrition intensified by the lack of medical attention.

Political prisoners, the author reminds us were not always treated so brutally in Cuba. When Fidel Castro was imprisoned following his attack on the Moncada barracks on July 26 / 1953, he was given good food, large and airy quarters, full mail privileges and even conjugal visits. Mr. Castro himself wrote of "many pleasant hours" Spent in an airy yard, of good dinners with Italian Chocolate for dessert and two baths a day. "They're going to, make me think I'm on vacation," he quipped or as a clever taunting remark in a letter. By his own account, Mr. Castro had plenty of water, electric lights, food, clean clothes and all for free. Here Fidel Castro had what the Bible calls a delicious life of pleasure. So when you do not recognize these blessings that you have received and don't pass on these blessings along to others who may have did you wrong but asked and begged for mercy and forgiveness or did not ask for mercy or forgiveness because they have criticized you for your evil deeds ---well then you will one day find a curse by God against the male and female whores of this world known as this Apostate Catholic Church or their Babylonian atheists or infidels who are against the Authorized King James Version Bible and God. Who are the wicked men and women of the Babylonian lifestyle who have or been obsessed with excessive sex and food and materialism and being greedy and selfish in a position of supreme Authority in this world who will then be cursed and judged by God for their evil deeds they have committed according to Revelation 18: 1, 2, 3, 4, 5, 6, 7, 8.

This story of "Tupac Shakur" of the rich and famous is one of intrigue and suspense of the final outcome of a story like this. Tupac Shakur, an American rapper, was fatally shot on September 7th / 1996, in a drive by shooting in the Las Vegas Valley, Nevada. He was 25 years old. The shooting occurred at 11: 15 p.m. (PDT), when the car carrying Shakur was stopped at a red light at East Flamingo Road and Koval lane.

Shakur was struck by four rounds fired from a .40 caliber Glock pistol that is a brand of polymer-framed, short recoil-operated, locked-breech (which reloads at near the rear portion of the gun barrel). Shakur was hit with two slugs in the chest and one in the arm, and one in the thigh. He died from his wounds six days later.

At the time of during the writing of this manuscript to this book called "Ancient of Blood of Violence" dated September 29th / 2023, Duane "Keefe D" Davis was arrested after being indicted by a grand jury for the first-degree murder of Tupac Shakur.

Tupac Shakur attended the " Bruce Seldon vs. Mike Tyson boxing match with Marion "Suge" Knight, the head of "Death Row Records", at the MGM Grand in Las Vegas, Nevada. After leaving the match, one of Knight's associates, Trevon "Tre" Lane, a member of the "M.O.B. Pirus" gang based in Compton, California, spotted Orlando " Baby Lane " Anderson, from the rival "South Side Compton Crips" Gang, in the MGM Grand lobby. Earlier that year, in July 1996, Orlando "Baby Lane" Anderson and a group of Southside Crips attempted to rob Trevon "Tre" Lane in a "Foot Locker" store at the "Lakewood Center" mall in Lakewood California.

Trevon "Tre" Lane told Shakur who in turn attacked Anderson in the Lobby. Shakur asked Anderson if he was from the "South" (Southside Crips) and punched him in the face, knocking him to the ground. Shakur and Knight's entourage assisted in assaulting Anderson. The fight which was captured on the MGM Grand video surveillance, and was broken up by hotel security.

After the brawl, Shakur returned to his hotel, the "Luxor Las Vegas." He disclosed to girlfriend Kidada Jones his involvement in the Anderson Fight, previously having promised to return to her after entering the MGM Grand and having her stay in a vehicle. Shakur left with Knight, in a BMW sedan after changing clothes and went to club 662, which was owned by Knight to perform at a charity concert.

At 11:00 - 11: 05 p.m. (PDT) Shakur and Knight were halted on Las Vegas Boulevard by officers from the "Las Vegas Metropolitan Police Department" Bike Patrol for playing the car stereo too loudly and not having license plates. The plates were found in the trunk of Knight's car. The party was released a few minutes later without being cited. At 11:10 p.m., while they were stopped at a red light at the intersection of East Flamingo Road and Koval lane in front of the Maxim Hotel, a vehicle occupied by two women pulled up on their left side. Shakur, who was talking through the window of his brand new 1996 BMW 750iL, exchanged words with the two women, and invited them to go to Club 662.

At 11: 15 p.m., a white, four door, late model Cadillac pulled up to Knight's right side. The shooter, seated at the back of the Cadillac, rolled down the window and rapidly fired gunshots from a .40 S&W glock 22 at Shakur's BMW. Shakur was hit four times: twice in the chest, once in the arm, once in the thigh. One of the bullets went into Shakur's right lung. Knight was hit in the head by fragmentation.

Shakur's bodyguard Frank Alexander stated that when he was about to ride along with Shakur in Knight's car, Shakur asked him to drive Jone's car instead, in case they needed additional vehicles from Club 662 back to their hotel. Alexander reported in his documentary, "Before I Wake", that shortly after the assault, one of the convoy's cars followed the assailant but he never heard from the occupants. Yaki Kadafi an American Rapper was riding in the car behind Shakur with bodyguards at the time of the shooting and, along with members of the Death Row entourage, who refused to cooperate with police.

Despite Knight's injuries, and his vehicle having a flat tire, he was able to drive Shakur and himself a mile from the site of the shooting, to Las Vegas Boulevard and Harmon Avenue. They were again pulled over by the Police Bike patrol, who alerted paramedics through radio. After arriving on the scene, police and paramedics took Knight and Shakur to the "University Medical Center of Southern Nevada." They were pulled over just a short distance from the MGM Grand, where their evening had begun.

Gobi Rahimi, a Death Row music video director who visited Shakur at the hospital, later reported that he received news from Death Row marketing employee that the shooters had called the record label and threatened Shakur. Gobi told Las Vegas police about this threat but police said they claimed to be understaffed. No attackers came to the hospital. Shakur said he was dying while being carried into the emergency room.

At the hospital, Shakur was heavily sedated, and was placed on life support machines, and was ultimately put under a medically induced coma after repeatedly trying to get out of bed. He was visited by Jones and regained consciousness when she played Don McLean's "Vincent" a song of tribute by Don McLean to Vincent van Gogh (an artist and his painting "The Starry Night " who died of an illness at age 27) on the CD player next to Shakur's hospital bed. According to Jones, Shakur moaned and his eyes were filled with "mucus and swollen." Jones told Shakur that she loved him.

Knight was released from the hospital the day following the shooting on September 8th, but did not speak until September 11th. He told officers he "heard something, but saw nothing " the night of the shooting. A spokesman for the officers said Knight's statement did nothing to help the investigation. Officers at the time of Shakur's hospitalization reported having no leads. Sgt. Kevin Manning said during the week that officers didn't receive "a whole of cooperation" from Shakur's entourage.

Rahimi and members of Shakur 's group "Outlawz" (a hip-hop group founded by rapper Tupac Shakur in late 1995 after Shakur's release from prison and arrival at Death Row Records) here the Outlawz guarded Shakur while he stayed in the hospital due to their fears that whoever shot Shakur "was gonna finish him off." Ramimi mentioned the possibility that Outlawz brought weapons with them. While in the critical care unit on the afternoon of Friday, September 13, 1996, Shakur died of respiratory failure that lead to cardiac arrest after the removal of his right lung. Doctors attempted to revive him. but could not stop the hemorrhaging. His mother "Afeni" (who was an American political activist and a member of the Black Panther Party. Afeni was also the executor of Tupac's Shakur estate. She founded the Tupac Amaru Shakur Foundation and also served as the CEO of Amaru Entertainment Inc., a record and film production company she founded. Tupac Shakur's mother Afeni made the decision to cease medical treatment. He was pronounced dead at 4: 03 p.m.

In 2014, A police officer who claimed he witnessed Shakur's last moments said that Shakur refused to state who shot him. When the officer asked Shakur if he saw the person or people who shot him, Shakur responded by saying "Fuck you" to the officer as his last words. Paramedics and other officers present at the scene did not report hearing Shakur say those words, nor did Knight or bodyguard Frank Alexander who were also present.

One year after the shooting, Sgt. Kevin Manning, who headed the investigation, told Las Vegas Sun investigative reporter Cathy Scott that Shakur's murder " may never be solved." The case slowed early in the investigation, he said as few new clues came in and witnesses clammed up. Manning stated that the investigation was at a standstill. Also "E.D.I. mean" a Hip Hop artist and a collaborator of Shakur's and a member of Outlawz, said he was positive law enforcement knew "what happened" added, "This is America. We found bin Laden."

In 2002, the los Angeles times published a two-part story by Chuck Philips, titled "Who Killed Tupac Shakur" based on a year-long investigation. Philips reported that " the shooting was carried out by a Compton gang called Southside Crips to avenge the beating of one of its members by Shakur a few hours earlier. Orlando Anderson, the Crip whom Shakur had attacked, fired the fatal shots. Las Vegas police considered Anderson as a suspect and interviewed him only once, briefly. Anderson was killed nearly two years later in an unrelated gang shooting. Philips's article implicated East Coast rappers, including "The Notorious B.I.G.," Tupac's rival at the time, and several New York City criminals.

The second Article in Philips series assessed the murder investigation and said that Las Vegas police had mismanaged the probe. His article enumerated the missteps of the Las Vegas police as follows:
1. Discounting the fight that occurred just hours before the shooting, in which Shakur was involved in beating Anderson in the MGM Grand lobby;
2. Failing to follow up with a Member of Shakur's entourage who witnessed the shooting, who told Las Vegas police he could probably identify one or more of the assailants, but was killed before being interviewed;
3. Failing to follow up a lead from a witness who spotted a white Cadillac similar to the car from which the fatal shots were fired and in which the shooters escaped.

Haaretz an Israeli newspaper, reported in 2011 that the FBI released documents, as a result of a "Freedom of Information Act" request, revealing its investigation of the "Jewish Defense League" for extorting protection money from Shakur and other rappers after making death threats against them. In 2017, Knight claimed he might have been the target of the attack that killed Shakur, arguing that it was a hit on him as a staged coup to seize control of Death Row Records. Here it is obvious that this was about greed and taking control of others and their money assets such as this record label of Death Row Records and perhaps looking to take control of other record labels much in the same way the Pharisees took control of Christ and accused him and arrested him and instead released Barabbas who was in prison and was a robber and had Christ crucified for the envy that the Jews had for Christ (Matthew 27: 17, 18) when he was claiming to be sent by God and to carry out a ministry for God that would lead him to rule the kingdom taking the place of the authority positions or leaderships of the Chief priests which were the Pharisees and the Jews in that ancient time of Christ according John 3 : 1, 2, 3, 4, 5, 6, 7, 8, 9, 10, 11, 12 and John 18 : 28, 29, 30, 31, 32, 33, 34, 35, 36, 37, 28, 39, 40.

I am not saying that Shakur had a similar character that a true Christian had in being faithful to Christ but Shakur may have sowed discord among and in the world of Hip Hop and Rappers and their affiliates and associates in the Hip Hop and Rapper underworld of Gangsters.

At the time of the shooting, an entourage of around ten automobiles were following Knight and Shakur's vehicle. The year following the shooting, Knight stated during an "ABC Primetime Live" interview that he did not know who had shot Shakur but would never tell officers even if he did know.

Kadafi was involved in a scuffle with officers two days following the shooting, after they pulled over a motorist he was acquainted with and he protested. Kadafi left Las Vegas days after Shakur's death traveling to Atlanta and Los Angeles before settling in New Jersey, Where his relatives lived. In that time Compton investigators assembled mug shots of several gang members, which included Anderson, and hand delivered them to Las Vegas. Manning said Detectives called Kadafi's lawyer to set up a meeting with the rappers so that he could be shown the pictures. According to Manning, the calls were not returned. Officers did not try to locate Kadafi, who was fatally shot in a housing project in Irvington, New Jersey, in November 1996, two months after Shakur's shooting.

E.D.I. Mean and bodyguard Frank Alexander told the "Times" in early 1997 that they had never been asked by Las Vegas police to view photos of possible suspects in the case, despite having observed the shooting and having seen the men in the car from which the shots were fired. In an interview with Alexander conducted by Las Vegas police on March 19th / 1997, he was shown a series of eight photo images, but was unable to identify any suspects from them. E.D.I. Mean claimed to have seen all four men in the vehicle, while Alexander reported seeing the face of the suspect who shot Shakur. In his March 1997 police interview, Alexander, said that he only saw the occupants of the shooter's car in "more of a profile." Las Vegas police disputed the pair's account of what they had reported to the officer's the night of the shooting.

In the "USA Network" documentary "Unsolved," broadcast in 2018, Duane " Keefe D " Davis, a Crips gang leader in California and Anderson's uncle, claimed to have been in the car, specifically in the front passenger seat, with Tupac's murderer when the shots were fired. He declined to name the shooter, citing "street code." Despite this, he stated that the car was driven by Terrence "T- Brown" Brown and that Anderson and DeAndrae "Dre" Smith were sitting in the backseat. In 2016 a M.O.B. Piru and former Death

Row Bodyguard named James "Mob" James McDonald claimed he saw Anderson and other Southside Crips pull near Club 662 in a white Cadillac and were briefly parked in the lot prior to the shooting of Suge's BMW. According to Radar Online, Keefe D stated that after waiting near Club 662, they went to a Liquor Barn store and they then proceeded to make their way to "The Carriage House" hotel. On their way there they noticed the Death Row caravan.

In 1993 while visiting Los Angeles "The Notorious B.I.G." asked a local Drug Dealer to introduce him to Shakur and they quickly became friends. The pair would socialize when Shakur went to New York or to B.I.G. in Los Angeles. During this period, at his own live shows Shakur would call B.I.G. onto stage to rap with him and stretch. Together they recorded the songs "Runnin from tha police" and "House of Pain." Reportedly, B.I.G. asked Shakur to Manage him, whereupon Shakur advised him that Sean Combs would make him a star. Yet in the meantime Shakur's lifestyle was comparatively lavish to B.I.G. who had yet established himself. Shakur welcomed B.I.G. to join his side group "Thug Life" but he would instead form his own side group, "The Junior M.A.F.I.A." with his Brooklyn friends Lil ' Cease and Lil' Kim. Shakur had a falling out with B.I.G. after he was shot at Quad Studios in 1994.

Shakur's third album "Me Against The World," was released while he was incarcerated in March 1995. It is now hailed as his Magnum Opus or possibly given critical praise and commonly ranks among the greatest most influential Rap albums. The album debuted at No. 1 on the Billboard 200 and sold 240,000 copies in its first week setting a then record for the highest first week sales for a solo male rapper. Shakur now best Rap Album at the 1996 Soul Train Music Awards. In 2001, it ranked 4th among his total Albums in sales, with about 3 million copies sold in the U.S.

While Shakur was imprisoned in 1995, his mother was about to lose her house. Shakur had his wife Keisha Morris contact Death Row Records founder Suge Knight in Los Angeles. Reportedly Shakur's mother promptly received 15,000 dollars. After an August visit to Clinton Correctional facility in northern New York state, Knight traveled southward to New York City to attend the 2nd Annual Source Awards ceremony. Meanwhile an east coast -west coast Hip Hop rivalry was brewing between Death Row Records and

Bad Boy Records. In October 1995, Knight visited Shakur in prison again and posted 1.4-million-dollar bond. Shakur returned to Los Angeles and joined Death Row Records with the appeal of his December 1994 conviction pending.

Shakur's fourth Album "All Eyez On Me" arrived on February 13th / 1996. It was Rap's first double Album --- meeting two or three Albums due in Shakur's contract with Death Row Records --- and bore five singles. The Album shows Shakur rapping about the Gangsta Lifestyle, Leaving behind his previous political messages. With standout production the Album has more party tracks and often a triumphant tone music Journalist Kevin Powell noted that Shakur, once released from prison became more aggressive and seemed like a completely transformed person. To make a long story short this aggressive behaviour on behalf of Shakur may have led to this Venomous Tirade --- the proclaimed " Bad Boy Killer " threatens violent pay back on all things Bad Boy , B.I.G., Sean Combs, Junior M.A.F.I.A., the company and on any in the east coast Rap scene like Rap Duo "Mobb Deep" and Rapper Chinoxl who allegedly had commented against Shakur about the dispute. Here Shakur may have caused discord in the midst the world of gangsters and spreading possibly threats in every direction which may have led to confusion and eventual violence that led and caused the assassination of other members of these gangs such as B.I.G., Kadafi, and Anderson the nephew of Duane "Keefe D" Davis who was arrested on September 29th / 2023 for the shooting of Tupac Shakur. In the back of a police cruiser Davis had a brief conversation with a police officer after his arrest where Davis was asked by the officer what he was doing in the back of the cruiser ---- Davis responded by mentioning the date of his offence which was the date of September 7th / 1996 which was the shooting of Shakur. The officer responded and as he was familiar with the date and said "No shit eh?" Then Davis responded and said "I didn't do shit" ---- then officer said "well that is what court is for." Here I can understand what Duane "Keefe D" Davis meant by this statement saying "I didn't do shit" which simply meant that Tupac Shakur may have sowed discord among the brethren of the gangster underworld that led to the deaths of Notorious BI.G., Kadafi, and Anderson according to Proverbs 6: 14 , 19 and Proverbs 16: 28, 29, 30. It is possible that these murders like Anderson's murder may have been unrelated here; but we may never know the truth here in regards to the silent and loyalty codes of the gangster underworld.

Here never under estimate anyone or overestimate your security in life by trying to impress a girlfriend by telling her you beat the shit out of someone who did you wrong in a minor incident; since Shakur's girlfriend may have told or bragged about this fight during months of July and August of 1996 through the grapevine in the bars or in the night clubs leading to, and resulting to the shooting death of Shakur on September 7th / 1996. Whether this revelation of this fight was revealed by Shakur's girlfriend in a boastful or bragging manner or not or it was done discreetly or not --- it is a very dangerous thing to reveal it at all, even by a less severe amount of slandering when you are involved and surrounded by people who have guns who have a lesser reputation than you do; and to be reckless after you have this recognition and fame and money that will not save you in the end and to believe that you have that right to beat someone to a pulp in numbers in a cowardly act like Shakur has done ---- and to do it when you may be a good fighter or not for the petty theft Anderson may have committed against Trevon " Tre " Lane is a recipe to become a target for the underworld of gangsters.

Also, these rival gangs may kill to make a mark and that to cross any of them was a death sentence especially cutting into the way they are dealing either in drugs or racketeering in a general sense. But it is not only about dealing in drugs and racketeering but the reputations and impressing the people around you, especially all the women who surround these gangsters, and to humiliate them through the grapevine whether on the street or in nightclubs or in the bar scene is a precarious thing to do in this underworld of gangsters.

 Here the Bible speaks of this attitude that was displayed in an arrogant and boastful manner by Shakur and his friends and girlfriends who surrounded him and that Shakur was especially popular with the girls and women in general not only on the street but in nightclubs and revered by the community of Celebrities and the public where you could be on the wrong side of what is right and what is wrong ---- and that to this reasoning there is a fine line between life and death. Here Shakur was rich and famous and may have not been humble and may have not been one to tolerate humility and therefore may have not been committed to intreat or negotiate or beg or plead since he answered the circumstances of this theft by Anderson that was done either against him or against his colleagues or friends in a rough manner thinking his fame and riches would save him and this in turn led to his death by the poor gangsters who used intreaties and that he had a girlfriend or wife that did not do him a favour by blabbing and shooting her mouth off disparaging these less prosperous and perhaps honest rival gangsters who were degraded by a pretty girlfriend or girlfriends of Shakur ruining these less prosperous gangster's reputations because of his fame and money and success that propelled his reputation to an overwhelming reputable state of affairs in the nightclubs and their societal grapevines ruining the reputation of these poor or less prosperous gangsters according to Proverbs 18: 12, 21, 22, 23, 24.

And furthermore, is that Shakur should have feared his boasting and feared having that foolish and raging confidence in destroying a person's reputation. And instead did not forgive Orlando Anderson "Baby Lane" but to humiliate him and the people he was involved with or who he knew who were these poor or less prosperous gangsters who were provoked in the end by Shakur's slandering comments he and his girlfriends may have made behind these poor and less prospering gangsters' backs and hiding his hatred for them and not having the guts to confront them face to face was an evil and hate waiting to happen to him resulting in his death by assassination according to Proverbs 14: 16, 17 and Proverbs 10: 18.

Speaking of Ancient Blood of Violence we have a Queen by the name Jezebel who was a treacherous woman and was also considered by most as a killer and a prostitute who may have lured her victims like Naboth to taking his vineyard and had him accused falsely of blaspheme against God and took his vineyard and had him stoned to death. Now as this story goes in the beginning Queen Jezebel got married to Ahab. Here Ahab was obsessed with Naboth's vineyard that he wanted the vineyard for his own. Ahab offered Naboth a better vineyard or offered him the worth of Naboth's vineyard in money. But Naboth refused saying that the Lord had forbid him to give him or sell him the vineyard and also to why should he give the inheritance of his fathers of this vineyard to Ahab? According to I Kings 21: 2, 3. After this Ahab was discouraged over the fact that Naboth would not give up his vineyard to him and so here Ahab became weak and depressed and troubled where he would not eat according to I Kings 21 : 4. Jezebel Ahab 's wife was a strong and determined woman who wanted to help Ahab her husband to possess this vineyard at any cost. Here Ahab was considered a weak man who was married to a strong willed and cunning and treacherous and wicked woman who would take no for an answer. After an unspecified amount of time had passed, since Ahab was notably rebuked by an unnamed prophet for letting Ben-Hadad survive (Ben-Hadad was the king of Aram-Damascus between 885 BCE and 865 BCE. Ben-Hadad planned to capture Ahab's "wives", including Jezebel, as plunder after besieging Samaria), he visited Naboth's residence. The residence was located near the royal palace in the city of Jezreel. Wishing to acquire Naboth's vineyard so that he could expand his own gardens, Ahab asked to purchase Naboth's vineyard in exchange for a better-quality vineyard or financial compensation. Naboth Declined, which he justified by informing Ahab that his vineyard was ancestral property. Ahab returned to his palace, sullen and depressed by Naboth's response. Jezebel decided to console him by arranging for Naboth to be entrapped and later executed on the false charges of blasphemy against God and the king. After Naboth was executed outside the city, his corpse was licked by stray dogs. And this story of Naboth's fate in this world of persecution and Ahab's fate; that has resulted in being given a burden, by and in the sight of God that is recorded in and according to 1st Kings 21: 1 to 29.

Jezebel then informed Ahab that he could seize Naboth's vineyard. Elijah condemned Ahab for committing theft and murder. As punishment, God decreed Ahab's death and the annihilation of his royal line. Three years later, Ahab died in battle. His son Ahaziah inherited the throne, but died as the result of an accident and Ahaziah was succeeded by his brother, Joram. Elisha, Elijah's successor, commanded one of his disciples to anoint Jehu, commander of Joram's army, as king, to be the agent of divine punishment against Ahab's family. Jehu killed Joram, and his nephew Ahaziah (the king of Judah and son of Athaliah, who was possibly the daughter of Jezebel). He later approached the royal palace in Jezreel to confront Jezebel.

Knowing that Jehu was coming, Jezebel put on make-up and a formal wig with adornments and looked out of a window, taunting him. Geoffrey W. Bromiley (an Ecclesiastical Historian Theologian, professor emeritus at fuller Theological Seminary) says that it should be looked at less an attempt at seduction than the public appearance of the queen mother, invested with the authority of the royal house and cult, confronting a rebellious commander. In his two volume Guide to the Bible (1967 and 1969), Isaac

Asimov describes Jezebel's last act: dressing in all her finery, make up, and jewelry as deliberately symbolic, indicating her dignity, royal status, and determination to go out of this life as a queen.

Jehu later ordered Jezebel's eunuch servants to throw her from the window. Her blood splattered on the wall and horses, and Jehu's horse trampled her corpse. He entered the palace where, after he ate and drank, he ordered Jezebel's body to be taken for burial. His servants discovered only her skull, her feet, and the palms of her hands - her flesh had been eaten by stray dogs, just as the prophet had prophesied. Edwin R. Thiele (An American Seventh - day Adventist missionary in China, editor, Archaeologist, writer, and scholar of the Old Testament) who dates Jezebel's death at c. 850 BCE., according to 2nd Kings 9 : 30 to 37.

Here the name " Jezebel " is use today as a term or the name " Jezebel " is closely associated with or to the immorality of a woman and her promiscuity or her promiscuous means to control others in scheming conspiracies for either fraud or murder or monetary gain or the unjustly convicted subjects punished by sexual assault and sexual servitude during the Black African American Slavery in the 1800's. The Jezebel Stereotype is an oppressive image and was used as a justification for sexual assault and sexual servitude during the eras of Colonization and Slavery in the United Sates.

Also, on August 8th / 2023 wildfires destroyed Maui and Lahaina communities in the State of Hawaii. These wildfires began on the hills above downtown Lahaina around sunrise on August 8th / 2023. Evidence suggests heavy winds downed power lines in the area, sending sparks into dry shrubland. Hawaiian Electric said this appears to have been the cause of the fire that morning of August 8th / 2023. Here the Kings and Queens of Hollywood like Mick Fleetwood's home was not touched by fire but his restaurant business was burnt to the ground or suffered severe damage. The Maui's Celebrities' Residents was a quiet place as the town was torched by fires. Owen Wilson 's home was not affected by these wildfires nor was the following Celebrities in Maui and Lahaina and the rest of the state of Hawaii like these Celebrities here like, Oprah Winfrey's land or Grand Wailea, Four Seasons Wailea, Steven Tyler's house, Jeff Bezo's 78-million-dollar home, Larry Ellison who owns 98% of Lanai. Also, Clint Eastwood's home was not affected by the wildfires either.

 Here why were these Celebrities off the hook and have not become victims of these wildfires? You know it does not make any sense for the wicked to sacrifice something to God like giving up food for fasting or giving up your home for your faith in God whether it is for repenting of your sins or simply suffering for Christ. So, having said this, a sacrifice by the wicked is an abomination to God so this scripture in Proverbs 15: 8 refers to the fact that God had those poor people or those of the middle class who were hard workers making only enough money to get by that were sacrificed by these wildfires. They may have not suffered judgment by God after they have been killed by these wildfires. Why do you think that firefighters die or those in war get killed? After they die and sacrifice their lives for God do you think they get judged? Or are they blessed for this sacrifice brought on by God and the winds that God brought to these wildfires where the wicked are not sacrificed because sacrificing a celebrity that mocks God or is not loyal to the word of God in the Authorized King James Version Bible is an abomination to God according to Galatians 6: 7 and Proverbs 15: 8 and Galatians 6: 7 and Job 37: 21, 22, 23, 24 and Jeremiah 21: 10, 11, 12, 13, 14. Amazing since these wildfires started in the morning according to Jeremiah 21: 12. But as we know by faith that these scriptures cover similar multiple circumstances regarding judgment on mankind by God and wildfires that happen here throughout the diverse places on planet earth.

CHAPTER 3
INCARCERATED SUICIDES & MURDERS

The ancient and historical killings in prison and the suicides in prison that have taken place are and have been incidents that have been a burden and a load to the Justice System. Where investigations take place because of a suicide or a murder in prison. This causes the government to spend more money for these investigations and inquiries. Money that could be used to rehabilitate prisoners or inmates and help these inmates reintegrate back into society. When a murder happens or a suicide happens there is the question as to who influenced or caused a suicide to happen or who committed the murder. In most cases the inmates may have committed murder. But there may be no cases that any prison guard in the present or in the past was ever charged with murder --- and if this is the case in our world of prisons this could be a rare incident or incidents that may have occurred where a prison guard is thought to have committed murder and been also charged and convicted. But those prison guards who were charged for negligence causing death is perhaps more common than we think.

Going back in history things may have been more negligence in a prison or a dungeon because of the lack of surveillance and the lack of camera surveillance that may have been a problem for authorities who were true to the treatment of prisoners and their human rights. One example is "Vercingetorix" during 46 BC who was a Gallic king and chieftain of the Averni tribe who united the Gauls. (that was a region of Western Europe first clearly described by the Romans, encompassing present- day France, Belgium, the Netherlands, Luxembourg and parts of Switzerland, Germany, and Northern Italy, it covered an area of 494,000 square Kilometers.) But it was a failed revolt against Roman forces during the last phase of Julius Caesar's Gallic Wars. Despite having willingly surrendered to Caesar, Vercingetorix was executed by strangulation in a prison in Rome and being detained at the time by the Roman Republic.

Another ancient blood of violence of incarcerated homicide that was not violent but came close to being violent and gruesome regarding being beheaded which is indeed a messy form of execution. Here he was tried and may had avoided the beheading that may have taken place of Philip Howard, who was Philip Howard, 13th Earl of Arundel Born June 28th / 1557 and was also an English nobleman. He was canonized by Pope Paul VI in 1970, as one of the Forty Martyrs of England and Wales. Howard lived mainly during the reign of Queen Elizabeth I.

He was charged with being a Catholic, quitting England without leave, and sharing in Jesuit plots known as being a member of the " Society of Jesus " whose members are known as the " Jesuits ", is a religious order of clerics regular of pontifical right for men in the Catholic Church headquartered in Rome. For this religious and political dissent, he was sent and imprisoned to the Tower of London in 1585. Philip Howard, 13th Earl of Arundel spent ten years in the Tower of London, until his death from "Dysentery." Historically known as the "bloody flux" which is a type of gastroenteritis that results in bloody diarrhea. Other symptoms may include fever, abdominal pain, and feeling of incomplete defecation. Complications may include dehydration.

Shortly after Philip Howard's birth, his mother became seriously ill, possibly from puerperal infection "a Postpartum infection or infections," also known as childbed fever and puerperal fever, are any bacterial infections of the female reproductive tract following childbirth or miscarriage. Signs and symptoms usually include a fever greater than 38.0 degrees C. (100.4 degrees F.), chills, lower abdominal pain, and possibly bad smelling vaginal discharge. It usually occurs after the first 24 hours and within the first ten days following delivery. Here if a woman has had more than one partner in sexual intercourse where they are no longer a Chaste Virgin, then they are no longer both holy in body and spirit if they don't repent and accept Christ and drinking the blood and water of Christ making them holy again after losing their Chaste virginity.

Here Pure Virginity or Chaste Virginity does not bring on these vaginal health complications such as bacterial infections of the female reproductive organs or tract. Where here after this --- multiple sexual intercourse with different sexual partners leaves them open to the infection and infecting sexual organs. And open to the corruption of the flesh and where a woman is open to be unholy spiritually --- and unholy in the flesh and blood of the body, and to the body's sexual organs. And the general fleshly defiled state of the body and spirit open to the vulnerability of infection to the body and to the corruption to the flesh and of not being both holy in body and in spirit according to 1st Corinthians 7: 32, 33, 34, 35, 36, 37, 38, 39 and Galatians 6: 8. Here Philip Howard's mother possibly died from this puerperal infection at Arundel House in August of that year.

Philip's father, a Roman Catholic with a Protestant education, was arrested in 1569 for being involved in intrigues against Queen Elizabeth I, mainly because of the Duke's intention to marry--- Mary, Queen of Scots. Although he was released in August 1570, a few months later he became involved in the Ridolfi Plot, being arrested again in September 1571 when his participation in the Ridolfi plot was discovered. He was executed in June 1572 when Philip Howard 13th Earl of Arundel was 15 years old and who was the son of Thomas Howard 4th Duke of Norfolk involved in the Ridolfi Plot (the Ridolfi Plot was a Roman Catholic plot in 1571 to kidnap or assassinate Queen Elizabeth I of England and replace her with Mary Queen of Scots. The plot was hatched and planned by Robert Ridolfi, an international banker who was able to travel between Brussels, Rome and Madrid to gather support without attracting too much suspicion). Thomas Howard, 4th Duke of Norfolk, a Roman Catholic with a Protestant education, and a cousin of Queen Elizabeth's and who was the wealthiest landowner in the country, had been proposed as a possible husband for Mary since her imprisonment in 1568.

This suited Duke of Norfolk, who had ambitions and felt Elizabeth persistently undervalued him. In pursuit of his goals, he agreed to support the Northern Rebellion known as a Revolt of the Northern Earls that was an unsuccessful attempt by the Catholic Nobles from Northern England to depose Queen Elizabeth I of England and replace her with Mary, Queen of Scots, though he quickly lost his nerve at this attempt to depose Queen Elizabeth. Here Thomas Howard 4th Duke of Norfolk was imprisoned in the Tower of London for nine months and only freed under house arrest when he confessed all and begged for mercy. Pope Puis V, in his 1570 papal bull Regnans in Excelsis (Reigning on high) excommunicated the Protestant Elizabeth and permitted all faithful Catholics to do all they could to dispose her. The Majority of English Catholics ignored the bull, but in response to it, Elizabeth Became much harsher to Catholics and their sympathizers.

Here Philip Howard 13th Earl of Arundel graduated in 1574, aged 17. He began attending Elizabeth I's court by the time he turned eighteen; notably, this was only a few years after his father Thomas Howard had been executed for treason against the Queen. His life had been frivolous both at Cambridge and remained so at court, where he nevertheless became a favourite of the Queen, despite Philip's troubled family past.
On September 30th / 1584, the Earl was also secretly received again into the Catholic Church by Jesuit priest Father William Weston. At the same time, the Earl's younger half - brother, Lord William Howard, was also received into Catholicism. Arundel, while still attending Elizabeth's court, successfully hid his adherence to Catholicism for a time, before withdrawing to his home and attempting to focus on being a better husband and father. The next year, Howard acted against Father Weston's cautions, by attempting to flee to mainland Europe in order to live openly as a Catholic with his wife and children.

His flight abroad was recommended, planned, and betrayed to Sir Francis Walsingham by a trusted servant, whom Father Philip Caraman identifies as the Earl's chaplain. He was an underground Catholic priest and agent provocateur Father Edward Grately. An "agent provocateur" is a person who commits, or acts to entice another person to commit, an illegal or rash act or falsely implicates them in partaking in an illegal act so as to ruin the reputation of, or entice legal action against, the target, or a group they belong to or are perceived to belong to. Here "recusants" who are still possibly now and were in the 1500's in a state of those who remained loyal to the Catholic Church. They refused to attend the Church of England services after the English Reformation.

Here these "recusants" had been able to successfully flee England, the Earl of Arundel, through his kinship to the late Anne Boleyn who was known as the Queen of England from 1533 to 1536, as the second wife of King Henry VIII. The circumstances of her marriage and of her execution by beheading for treason and other charges like adultery, incest and plotting to kill the King were viewed by historians regarding these charges as unconvincing. Here it made her a key figure in the political and religious upheaval that marked the start of the English Reformation; which included the Roman

Catholic Church as being labelled as a religious institution of Apostasy.

Here therefore the Earl of Arundel through his kinship to the late Anne Boleyn was a second cousin once removed by the Queen. He was widely considered by persecuted Roman Catholics who were plotting regime change to be a possible heir presumptive to the English throne. The Earl's ship was accordingly boarded by the Tudor Navy. (The Tudor Navy was the navy of the Kingdom of England under the ruling Tudor dynasty from 1485 to 1603. The period involved important and critical changes that led to the establishment of a permanent navy and laid the foundations for the future Royal Navy). While Earl's ship was setting sail from Littlehampton, it was accordingly boarded by the Tudor Navy where he was arrested and committed to the Tower of London on April 25th / 1585.

He was charged before the Star Chamber with being a Catholic, quitting England without leave, sharing in Jesuit plots, and claiming the title Duke of Norfolk in defiance of his Father's attainder. In English criminal law, attainder was the metaphorical "stain" or "corruption of blood" which arose from being condemned for a serious capital crime. It entailed losing not only one's life, and property and hereditary titles, but typically also the right to pass them on to one's heirs of both men and women. In other words, here Philip Howard, the 13th Earl of Arundel claimed the title of Duke of Norfolk in defiance of his Father's corrupt title of the Duke of Norfolk.

On May 17th / 1586 Philip Howard 13th of Earl of Arundel was fined 10,000 pounds and sentenced to imprisonment at the Queen's pleasure. In July 1586 he was offered his freedom if he would carry the sword of state before the Queen to church; he refused. Here humility on his behalf was not acted upon regarding his situation and therefore before his destruction and death his heart was and became haughty according to Proverbs 18: 12. In 1588 he was accused of praying, together with other Catholics, for the victory of the Spanish Armada. Here he was tried for high treason and on April 14th / 1589 and was found guilty. He was immediately condemned to death and attainted, with all his titles and property declared forfeit to the Crown. In a letter dated May 1st / 1589 to Claudio Aquaviva, Father Henry Garnet recalled, "When the sentence was pronounced and the crowd saw the Earl coming out of the hall with the axe-edge turned in towards him -- in the trial of nobles this is the sign that the prisoner has been condemned-- suddenly there was a great uproar that was carried miles along the river bank, some people demanding what had come of the Queen's clemency that such a splendid and gallant gentleman should suffer condemnation, others passionately indignant that a man who had prayed to God should be executed for that alone. For among the accusations brought against him, the principal charge and the one on which the whole case turned, -- was this --- he had asked a certain priest to pray for the success of the Spanish fleet. Whereas in fact, all his enemies could prove against him and all he had done was this, that he sought that prayers should be said every day and night in the Tower of London and in other prisons at that time, chiefly, when everyone was expecting a general massacre of Catholics. Queen Elizabeth did not sign his death warrant, but Philip Howard was never told this. He was constantly in fear of execution.

Here the Spanish Armada was commanded by Spanish aristocrat Alonso Perez' de Guzman y de Zuniga- Sotomayor, 7th Duke of Medina Sidonia GE where here the Spanish Armada was to attack the south of England. The 7th Duke of Medina Sidonia an aristocrat without naval experience where his orders were to sail up the English Channel, link up with the Duke of Parma in Flanders, and escort an invasion force that would land in England and overthrow Elizabeth I.

Its purpose was to reinstate Catholicism in England, end support for the Dutch Republic, and prevent attacks by English and Dutch privateers (or private civilians or vessels owned by them to aid in the conflict of war) against the Spanish interests in the Americas like North and South America or as known as the new world in that period of history in the 1500's or earlier. The Spanish were opposed by an English fleet based in Plymouth. Faster and more maneuverable than the larger Spanish galleons. They were able to attack the Armada as it sailed up the Channel. Several subordinates advised Medina Sidonia to anchor in The Solent and occupy the Isle of Wight, but he refused to deviate from his instructions to link up with Parma. Although the Armada reached Calais largely intact, while awaiting communication from Parma, it was attacked at night by English fire ships and forced to scatter.

The Armada suffered further losses in the ensuing Battle of Gravelines, and was in danger of running aground on the Dutch coast when the wind changed, allowing it to escape into the North Sea. Pursed by the English, the Spanish ships returned home via Scotland and Ireland. Up to 24 ships were wrecked along the way before the rest managed to get home. The expedition was the largest engagement of the undeclared Anglo-Spanish War. The following year, England organized a similar large-scale campaign against Spain, the English Armada, sometimes called the "counter- Armada of 1589" which was also a failure for the Spanish.

Here was Catholicism during the 1500's trying serve Christ truthfully? Like some who may be guilty of not being faithful to the word of God, regarding not the sins we commit --- but of not being truthful to the word of prophecy that God has revealed in his word? Like most Catholics today are not faithful to the prophecies of Revelation Chapter 17 mentioning the worldwide Catholic Church and its religious apostasy. Here these warnings from the word of God of Catholicism being apostate in nature is totally ignored by most Catholics or infidels of the Bible, or others who have different religious beliefs of having different views on who God truly is? And being involved in other religious institutions and denominations aside from Catholicism? One day Philip Howard scratched into a wall of his cell the words, still visible today in Latin; "Quanto plus afflictiones pro Christo in hoc saeculo, tanto plus gloriae cum Christo in futuro" here translated "The more affliction we endure for Christ in this world, the more glory we shall obtain with Christ in the next" (cf. Romans, chapter 8). Each day he spent several hours in prayer and meditation: he was noted for his patience in suffering and courtesy to unkind keepers. Was Philip Howard too enthusiastic about his faith in God? Where he may have been foolish, and has he over shot his mark of faith in God? Since what did he accomplish in history through his death? According to dying before his time at age 38, according to Ecclesiastes 7: 16, 17?

Death Row inmate Jonathan Fajardo was fatally stabbed by a fellow inmate at San Quentin State Prison on October 6th / 2018. It was the first murder of a condemned inmate in the U.S. in more than 20 years since 2018. Jonathon Fajardo, 30, was stabbed in the chest and neck with a makeshift weapon in the recreational yard at San Quentin as mentioned by a spokesperson named Terry Thornton. Luis Rodriguez, 34, was named as the alleged murder suspect. Investigators tried to determine a motive and how the suspect was able to obtain or make the weapon. Prison killings are rare on death row --- the last one occurred in 1997.

Jonathon Fajardo, 30 was stabbed in the chest and neck with an inmate made or fabricated or furbished weapon in a recreational yard of the cell house that holds the bulk of condemned inmates at the prison, Terry Thornton a corrections department spokeswoman told The Associated Press.

Fajardo was convicted in 2010 of first-degree murder in the fatal shooting of Cheryl Green, who's slaying a jury found was a hate crime motivated by her race. Fajardo was also convicted of participating in the death of 21-year-old Christopher Ash, a fellow gang member who prosecutors said was killed because he was suspected of talking to police about Green's killing. Fajardo was a member of the 204th Street gang; a Latino gang that prosecutors said intimidated and attacked African- Americans in the Harbor Gateway area of Los Angeles. Most of the victims were not affiliated with a gang, police said. According to court testimony, Fajardo walked up and opened fire on a group of young black people hanging out in a driveway December 15th / 2006. Green was killed and three others were injured in the unprovoked attack. Christopher Ash's body, stabbed more than 60 times, and with his throat slit, was found on the side of a road in Carson two weeks after Greens death.

Fajardo later admitted to police that he shot Green but called it an accident, saying he was aiming for a group of black men standing nearby. He told police that he and other gang members had earlier approached a sport utility vehicle driven by a black man, who pulled a gun as they came near, then drove off. The violence highlighted the racial tensions that had plagued the working- class community for a decade.

Fajardo, who was 18 when he shot and killed Green, was "cavalier" or thought the issue of Green's murder was considered unworthy or not important enough to sing during police interviews and warned that the gun used in the attack was still out there and could be used to kill other blacks, police, rival gang members or snitches, prosecutors said at the time.

Green's death sparked demonstrations and protests from residents and community activists. Black residents told the Los Angeles Times that they were often harassed and beaten by members of the 204th Street gang, and could not even patronize the area's only market, which the gang used as its hangout.

Within weeks of Green's slaying, then FBI Director Robert Mueller joined then-Mayor Antonio Villaraigosa and then-Police Chief William J. Bratton at a news conference in front of the market vowing to eradicate gang violence in the neighborhood.

Here even police officers and possibly Magistrates and Judges and Prosecutors in the justice system face a constant threat from terrorist activity from organized crime such as gangs or the mob or criminal syndicates that this is a Judgment of God for the transgressions of man on both sides of the law of those who make the laws in the legislature appointing judges and those who desire to break these laws who are threaten by criminals and criminal syndicates where judges, magistrates, prosecutors are assassinated or cut off for their sins as well according to Amos 2: 1, 2, 3.

There has been murders in prisons going back to the time of Christ and before these ancient times. Even today after all the contraband that we have where these guidelines and implementations are to keep brutal violence out of the hands of prison inmates. Contraband is not always a mechanism to prevent blood shed in a prison. Prisoners are checked for anything that may be an improvisation tool to make or furbish or fabricate a weapon. Usually these tools may be intricate and small enough to conceal up the rectum of an inmate wrapped in plastic. Where here Contraband checks are futile. Drugs are also concealed this way as well. Whether this is true I have no idea because I have only heard rumours or seen documented sources on the contraband of the prison system since I only spent time in the psychiatric system here in Ontario, Canada. Being in the penitentiary is always a learning experience and sometimes a lesson taught could be fatal. I for one would not survive the penitentiary even when you fight back it is true that you get respect for it by other inmates. But to back down in a fight which I am guilty of is a sure way of being killed ---- so either fight and get a broken jaw and missing teeth or die at the hands of reputable prison inmates.

Theobald Wolfe Tone posthumously known or we are born after the death of a father as Wolfe Tone who was known to be a father of reform for the accountability of government who died November 19th / 1798. Wolfe Tone was a leading Irish revolutionary figure and one of the founding members in Belfast and Dublin of the United Irishmen, a republican society determined to end British rule, and achieve accountable government, in Ireland. Throughout his political career, Tone was involved in a number of military engagements against the British navy. He was active in drawing Irish Catholics and Protestants together in the United cause, and in soliciting French assistance for a general insurrection. In November 1798, on his second attempt to land in Ireland with French troops and supplies, he was captured by British navy forces. The United Irish risings of the summer had already been crushed. Tone died in advance of his scheduled execution, probably, as modern scholars generally believe, by his own hand. Later generations were to regard Tone as the father of Irish Republicanism. His grave in Bodenstown, County Kildare, is the site of annual commemorations.

Wolfe Tone was born on June 20th / 1763. His father descended from a Huguenot family who were a religious group of French Protestants who held to the Reformed, or Calvinist, tradition of Protestantism. The Huguenot family fled to England from Gascony in the 16th century to escape religious persecution. A branch of the family settled in Dublin in the 17th century. Theobald's father Peter Tone, was a coachmaker who had a farm near Sallins, County Kildare and belonged to the Church of England. His mother, Margaret Lamport, came from a Catholic merchant family who converted to Protestantism after Theobald was born. His maternal grandfather was the captain of a vessel in the West India trade. He was baptized as Theobald Wolfe Tone in honour of his godfather. In the denominations of Christianity, a godparent is someone who bears witness to a child's baptism known also as christening and later is willing to help in their catechesis or to give oral instruction to the child as well as their lifelong spiritual formation. In the past, in some countries, the role carried some legal obligations as well as some religious guidelines.

In 1783, Tone found work as a tutor to Anthony and Robert, the younger half-brothers of Richard Martin MP of Galway, a prominent supporter of Catholic emancipation, at Dangan, the Martin family home. Tone fell in love with Martin's wife, but later wrote that it came to nothing. During this period, he briefly considered a career in theatre as an actor. As a student member at the Middle Temple in London he eloped with Martha Witherington, daughter of William and Catherine Witherington (nee Fanning) of Dublin. She would go on to change her name to Matilda, at Tone's request. When they married, Tone was 22, and Matilda was about 16. In 1796, while he was in France and she in Hamburg he wrote in his journal: " She is the delight of my eyes, the joy of my heart, the only object for which I wish to live. I dote upon her to distraction. Here Wolfe Tone was a man to either live for what was right or to die for what life offered that was wrong. Where life got deprived from this moral righteousness that he had sought for regarding the accountability of government according to Proverbs 15: 22 and Proverbs 24: 6.

Here Also in 1794, the United Irishmen, persuaded that no party in the Dublin parliament where being an MP was a limited to Anglicans; seemed likely to accept their scheme of universal manhood suffrage or electing a person for office or trust and equal electoral districts. And then when this had failed some, like Wolfe Tone began to recast their hopes on a French invasion due to the fact of this government corruption that was electing officials not fit for office. An Irish clergyman living in England, the Reverend William Jackson, who had taken in revolutionary opinions during his long stay in France, came to Ireland to ascertain to what extent the Irish people were ready to support a French invasion. Wolfe Tone drew up a memorandum for Jackson on the state of Ireland, which he described as ripe for a revolution. An attorney named Cockayne, to whom Jackson had imprudently or foolishly disclosed his mission, betrayed this memorandum to the government. In April 1794 Jackson was arrested on a charge of treason and dramatically committed suicide during his trial. So here there are a majority of lawyers or attorneys not only in ancient times or in history but also in our present period in our world that have gone and betrayed and plotted against the God of the Authorized King James Version Bible and against those who seek or have sought the Justice of this God of the Authorized King James Version Bible according to Luke 7 : 30 and Luke 11: 45, 46, 47, 48, 49, 50, 51, 52, 53, 54.

Summarizing his purpose of this French Invasion and revolutionary purpose and violence Tone declared the following:

To subvert the tranny of our execrable government, to break the connection with England, (the never failing source of our political evils) and to assert the independence of my country --- these were my objects. To unite the whole people of Ireland to abolish the memory of all past dissentions; and to substitute the common name of Irishmen in place of the denomination of Protestant, Catholic and Dissenter --- these were my means.

Yet he conceded that he "despaired" of Protestants (i.e. the Anglican Ascendancy) "for obvious reasons" they were already in possession of the whole power and patronage of the country. Appearing to "write off own class completely" in conversations with General Henri Clarke (a second-generation Irishman who later was to serve Napoleon as Minister of War) he apprehended a general massacre of the gentry and a redistribution of their entire property. The violence he would seek to restrain. On this score Hoche cautioned him not to be complacent. Tone records in his Memoirs:

Louis Lazare Hoche who Tone served for some months in the French army under Hoche who had become the French Republican's minister of war after his victory against the Austrians at the Battle of Neuwied on the Rhine in April 1797, here Hoche mentioned, also, that great mischief had been done to the principles of liberty and additional difficulties thrown in the way of the French Revolution, by the quantity of blood spilled: " for," he added, "if you guillotine a man, you get rid of an individual, it is true, but then you make all his friends and connections enemies forever of the government."

Tone expressed himself "heartily glad to find Hoche of this humane temperament" and trusted "we shall be able to avoid unnecessary bloodshed in Ireland."

What did Wolfe Tone mean by these comments? That to guillotine an innocent man who was for a good cause would not make whatever friends and connections he would have; that would be more favorable towards the government; that it would make his friends and connections become enemies of the Government.

When the prisoners were landed a fortnight later, Sir George Hill recognized

Tone in the French adjutant-general's uniform in Lord Cavan's privy-quarters at Letterkenny. At his trial by court-martial in Dublin on November 8th / 1798 Tone made a speech avowing his determined hostility to England and his intention "by frank and open war to procure the separation of the countries." Recognizing that the court was certain to convict him, he asked that: "the court should adjudge me to die the death of a soldier, and that I may be shot." Reading from a prepared speech, he defended his view of a military separation from Britain (as had occurred in the newly found and discovered place of North America being the fledgling United States) and explained his motives:

I entered into the service of the French Republic with the sole view of being useful to my country. To contend against British Tyranny. I have braved the fatigues and terrors of the field of battle; I have sacrificed my comfort, have courted poverty, have left my wife unprotected, and my children without a father. After all I have done for a sacred cause, death is no sacrifice. In such enterprises, everything depends on success. Washington Succeeded - Kosciusko failed. I know my fate, but neither ask for pardon nor do I complain. I admit openly all I have said, written, and done, and am prepared to meet the consequences.

As, however, I occupy a high grade in the French army, I would request that the court, if they can, grant me the favour that I may die the death of a soldier.

His eloquence was in vain, and his request to be shot was denied. On November 10th / 1798, he was found guilty and sentenced to be hanged on November 12th / 1798. Before this sentence was carried out, he was mortally wounded as a result either of being tortured by British soldiers or, as is today more generally accepted, of attempting to slit his own throat. The story goes that he was initially saved when the wound was sealed with a bandage, and he was told if he tried to talk the wound would open and he would bleed to death. He responded by saying "I cannot" yet find words to thank you sir; it is the most welcome news you could give me. What should I wish to live for? But Military surgeon Benjamin Lentaigne treated Tone just hours before he was due to be hanged. A pamphlet published in Latin by the doctor some years after Tone's official "suicide" refers to an unusual neck wound suffered by an unnamed patient which indicated that "a bullet passed through his throat." This has led to speculation that Tone may have been shot.

And so, Theobald Wolfe Tone who may or may not have died of suicide had according to sources died on November 19th / 1798 at age of 35 in Provost's Prison. Theobald Wolfe Tone had certainly hope in his death according to Proverbs 14: 32. Here Tone was a man who put forth an effort to establish his country and perhaps putting forth an effort to implement and influence that peace and justice of the God of the Authorized King James Version Bible. But he perhaps knew full well that this effort was in vain because there were too many people who would not support the justice that Christ spoke of where this kingdom that he was dealing with in this world was not of God. But of Satan who most people followed; and these people who were in numbers being the God of this world created the injustices that Tone was trying to eradicate. But failed because Christ had said that if it were his kingdom his servants would fight in order to secure his kingdom.

But Tone failed to take heed of Christ's warning here of the futile efforts that would come about and arise without the power of God and the prophetic destiny that God would influence later to bring into this world under the Divine rule of Christ and that his servants few in numbers presently, could neither fight nor abolish the governments of the Gentiles influenced by Satan and his deception. And by those who are deceived to follow Satan's perniciously apostate religious political and societal ways of all these people being infidels of the Authorized King James Version Bible and being the god of this world and deceiving the whole world. Here Satan brought his deception and influence, and coming as an angel of light which really refers to the darkness of anarchy, violence, crime, wars, deception and hatred which has brought on all the atrocities in our government and the world according to 2nd Corinthians 4: 4 and 2nd Corinthians 11: 13, 14, 15 and Luke 21: 8, 9, 10 and 2nd Timothy 3: 1, 2, 3, 4, 5 and John 18: 36 and Psalms 82: 2 and Ecclesiastes 5: 8, 9.

Hermann Wilhelm Goring from January 12th / 1893 to October 15th / 1946 was a German politician, military leader, and convicted war criminal. He was one of the most powerful figures in the Nazi Party, which ruled Germany from 1933 to 1945. A veteran World War I fighter pilot "ace," credited with shooting down five or more enemy aircraft Goring who was a recipient of the "Pour le Merite" (" The Blue Max "). He was the last commander of Jagdgeschwader 1 (JG I), the fighter wing once led by Manfred von Richthofen. An early member of the Nazi Party, Goring was among those wounded in Adolf Hitler's failed "Beer Hall Putsch" which was a failed coup d'etat by Nazi Party Leader Adolf Hitler in 1923. While receiving treatment for his injuries, he developed an addiction to morphine which persisted until the last year of his life. After Hitler became Chancellor of Germany in 1933, Goring was named as "minister without portfolio" in this new government who is either a government minister with no specific responsibilities or a minister who does not head a particular ministry. One of his first acts as a cabinet minister was to oversee the creation of the of the "Geheime Staatspolizei" also known abbreviated as the "Gestapo " which was the official secret police of Nazi Germany and German-occupied Europe. Here Goring ceded to or assigned to Heinrich Himmler in 1934. Here Heinrich Luitpold Himmler was the "Reichsfuhrer of the Schutzstaffel", a leading member of the Nazi Party, and one of the most powerful men in Nazi Germany, primarily known for being a main architect of the Holocaust.

Following the establishment of the Nazi state, Goring amassed power and political capital to become the second most powerful man in Germany. He was appointed commander-in-chief of the "Luftwaffe" (air force), a position he held until the final days of the regime. Upon being named "Plenipotentiary" which refers to a person of diplomatic status who is granted full powers of authorization which was also of the four-year plan which was a series of economic measures initiated by Adolf Hitler in Nazi Germany in 1936. Here Goring was entrusted with the task of mobilizing all sectors of the economy for war, an assignment which brought numerous government agencies under his control. In September 1939, Hitler gave a speech to the "Reichstag" designating him as his successor. After the fall of France in 1940, he bestowed the specially created rank of "Reichsmarschall" which is a rank and the highest military office in the "Wehrmacht" specially created for Hermann Goring during World War II. Here it also gave him seniority over all officers in Germany's armed forces. By 1941, Goring was at the peak of his power and influence. As the Second World War progressed, Goring's standing with Hitler and with the German public declined after the Luftwaffe proved incapable of preventing the

Allied bombing of Germany's cities and resupplying surrounded Axis Forces in Stalingrad. Around that time, Goring increasingly withdrew from military and political affairs to devote his attention to collecting property and artwork, much of which was stolen from Jewish victims of the Holocaust. Informed on April 22nd / 1945 that Hitler intended to commit suicide, Goring sent a telegram to Hitler requesting his permission to assume leadership of the Reich. Considering his request an act of treason, Hitler removed Goring from all his positions, expelled him from the party, and ordered his arrest. After the war, Goring was convicted of conspiracy, crimes against peace, war crimes, and crimes against humanity at the Nuremberg trials that took place in 1946 that were held by the Allies against representatives of the defeated Nazi Germany for plotting and carrying out invasions of other countries and atrocities against their citizens in World War II that ended on September 2 / 1945. He was sentenced to death by hanging but committed suicide by ingesting cyanide hours before the sentence was to be carried out.

Here we have man that brings evil to humanity because the evil he does goes unpunished for a more longer period than a sentence that is executed speedily therefore man is set in his own ways to do evil further. Where being hindered by these evil atrocities committed against humanity has carried on without a conscience and brought on more suffering to not only the innocent but the perpetrators of these war crimes. That here the fear that man does not have toward the God of the Authorized King James Version Bible. Where here the lack of conscience that man possesses is a common tragedy in our world that spawns in man a weak conscience and a foolish neglect to recognize to have fear towards committing atrocities and a genuine reverential fear towards God. Here men wages war one against the other for the righteous works and duties that righteous men try to accomplish verses the evil works and duties that the wicked try to accomplish against the righteous according to Ecclesiastes 8: 9, 10, 11, 12, 13, 14.

Richard Trenton Chase (May 23, 1950 - December 26, 1980) was an American serial killer, cannibal, and necrophile which refers to sexual attraction to a corpse. Here Richard Trenton Chase killed six people in the span of a month in 1977 and 1978 in Sacramento, California. He was nicknamed "The Vampire of Sacramento" because he drank his victims' blood and cannibalized their remains. Chase was a native of Sacramento, California. By the age of 5, he exhibited all three parts of the " Macdonald triad " which is known as a set of three factors, the presence of any two of which are considered to be predictive of, or associated with, violent tendencies, particularly with relation to serial offenses. The "triad" was first proposed by psychiatrist J.M. Macdonald in "The threat to kill" in a 1963 article. The "Macdonald triad" is a theory suggesting the development of violent psychopathy. In his adolescence he was a heavy drug user.

Chase developed hypochondria as he matured. He often complained that his heart would occasionally "stop beating", or that " someone had stolen his pulmonary artery an artery involved in the function of your heart. He would hold oranges on his head, believing Vitamin C would be absorbed by his brain via diffusion where the Vitamin C would be absorbed from a higher concentration area and transferred to a lower concentration area. Chase also believed that his cranial bones or his skull bones had become separated and were moving around, so he shaved his head to be able to watch this activity.

Chase spent a brief time in a psychiatric ward in 1973. In 1976 he was involuntarily committed to a mental institution when he was taken to a hospital after injecting rabbit's blood into his veins. The staff nicked named him "Dracula" because of his blood fixation. He broke the necks of two birds he caught through the institution window and drank their blood. He also extracted blood from therapy dogs with stolen syringes.

Chase was diagnosed with "paranoid schizophrenia." After undergoing a battery of treatments involving psychotropic drugs, Chase was deemed no longer a danger to society and later in 1976, he was released to his mother's custody. Chase's mother weaned him off his medication and got him his own apartment. He initially shared the apartment with roommates before all of them moved out, leaving Chase on his own. Later an investigation uncovered that, in mid-1977, Chase was stopped and arrested on a reservation in the Pyramid Lake, Nevada, area. His body was smeared with blood and a bucket of blood was found in his truck. The blood was determined to be cow's blood, and no charges were filed.

On December 29th / 1977, Chase killed his first known victim in a drive by shooting. The victim Ambrose Griffin, was a 51-year-old engineer and father of two. Two weeks later he attempted to enter the home of a woman, but because her doors were locked, he walked away. Chase later told detectives that he took locked doors as a sign he was not welcome, but unlocked doors were an invitation to come inside. On one occasion, he was caught and chased off by a couple returning home as he pilfered their belongings or to steal them in small amounts repeatedly. He had also urinated and defecated on their infant child's bed and clothing.

On January 23rd / 1978, Chase broke into a house and shot Teresa Wallin three times who was three months pregnant at the time. He then had "sexual intercourse with her corpses" an act known as "Necrophilia" while having this intercourse with her corpse he was at the same time stabbing her. He then removed multiple organs, and cut off one of her nipples and drank her blood. He stuffed dog feces from Wallin's yard down her throat before leaving.

On January 27, Chase entered the home of 38-year-old Evelyn Miroth. He encountered her friend Danny Meredith, whom he shot with his .22 handgun. He then fatally shot Miroth, her six-year-old son Jason, and her 22-month-old Nephew David Ferreira, before mutilating Miroth and engaging in necrophilia and cannibalism with her corpse. A visitor's knock on the door startled Chase, who fled in Meredith's car, taking Ferreira's body with him. The visitor alerted a neighbour, who called the police. They discovered that chase had left complete handprints and shoe imprints in Miroth's blood. Chase was arrested shortly afterwards; police who searched Chase's apartment found that the walls, floor, ceiling, refrigerator and all of Chase's eating and drinking utensils were soaked in blood.

In 1979, Chase stood trial on six counts of murder. in order to avoid the death penalty, the defense tried to have him found guilty of second-degree murder, which would result in a life sentence. Their case hinged on Chase's history of mental illness and the suggestion that his crimes were not premeditated or to think of and deliberately planned out thoroughly.
On May 8 1979, the jury found Chase guilty of six counts of first-degree murder and, rejecting the argument that he was not guilty by reason of insanity, the court sentenced him to die in the gas chamber. His fellow

inmates, aware of the extremely violent and grisly nature of Chase's crimes, feared him and, according to prison officials, often tried to persuade Chase to commit suicide.

Chase granted a series of interviews with Robert K. Ressler who was an FBI agent and author. He played a significant role in the profiling of violent offenders in the 1970's and is often credited with coining the term "serial killer" though the term is a direct translation of the German term "Serienmorder" coined in 1930 by Berlin investigator Ernest Gennat. After retiring from the FBI, he authored a number of books on serial murders, and often gave lectures on criminology. Chase during these series of interviews with Ressler, Chase spoke of his fears of Nazis and UFOs, claiming that although he had killed, it was not his fault; he had been forced to kill to keep himself alive, which he believed any person would do. He asked Ressler to give him access to a radar gun, with which he could apprehend the Nazi UFOs, so that the Nazi could stand trial for the murders. He also handed Ressler a large amount of macaroni and cheese, which he had been hoarding in his pants pockets, believing that the prison officials were in league with the Nazi and attempting to kill him with poisoned food.

Here if his fears of Nazis and UFO's was his only big problem ---- there is an entity much more devastating and much more frightening. Our Creator has that recognition of awe by the spiritually prudent people who place their trust in this Creator and his sovereignty of an all-powerful omnipresent, omnipotent, omniscient, omnipotence, and omnificent which means having infinite knowledge, infinite creative power, unlimited authority and influence, and having or possessing unlimited presence everywhere at the same time. Yes, this power is frightening indeed for those who commit atrocities or the rejection of the man who suffered severely for offering our redemption and eternal life and to offer that deliverance from our sin that spawns God's Judgment against us and casts us into an eternal hell. Yes, it is fearful to fall into the hands of this eternally living entity called God or to put it sarcastically mild here as the Bible points out in and according to Hebrews 10: 29, 30, 31. On December 26th / 1980, Chase was found dead in his prison cell. An autopsy revealed that he killed himself with an overdose of prescribed medications.

Jeffrey Lionel Dahmer (May 21st / 1960 to November 28 / 1994), also known as the Milwaukee Cannibal or the Milwaukee Monster, who was an American serial killer and sex offender who killed and dismembered seventeen males between 1978 and 1991. Many of his later murders involved necrophilia, cannibalism, and the permanent preservation of body parts --- typically all or part of the skeleton. Although he was diagnosed with borderline personality disorder (BPD), schizotypal personality disorder (StPD), and psychotic disorder, Dahmer was found to be legally sane at his trial. He was convicted of fifteen of the sixteen homicides he had committed in Wisconsin and was sentenced to fifteen terms of life imprisonment on February 17th / 1992. Dahmer was later sentenced to a sixteenth of life imprisonment for an additional homicide in Ohio in 1978.

Jeffrey Dahmer grew up in a troubled household. As Dahmer entered first grade. His father Lionel Herbert Dahmer kept him away from home much of the time due to his studies as a Marquette University Chemistry student and later became a research chemist due to research as a chemist he was away from home most of the time. When he was home his wife Joyce Annette Dahmer -- a hypochondriac who suffered from depression demanded constant attention and spent an increasing amount of time in bed. On one occasion, she attempted suicide using "Equanil" a drug known to be a tranquilizer. Consequently, neither parent devoted much time to their son Jeffrey, who later recollected that, from an early age, he felt "unsure of the solidity of the family," recalling extreme tension and numerous arguments between his parents during his early years. Dahmer had been an "energetic and happy child" but became notably subdued after "double hernia" surgery shortly before his fourth birthday. At elementary school, Dahmer was regarded as quiet and timid; one teacher recollected she detected early signs of abandonment due to his father's absence and his mother's illnesses, the symptoms of which increased when she became pregnant with her second child. In elementary school Dahmer had a small number of friends.

From an early age, Dahmer manifested an interest in dead animals. His fascination with dead animals may have begun when, at the age of four, he saw his father removing animal bones from beneath the family home. According to his father Lionel Dahmer his son Jeffrey was "oddly thrilled" by the sound the bones made, and became preoccupied with animal bones, which he initially called his "fiddlesticks." He occasionally searched beneath and around the family home for additional bones, and explored the bodies of live animals to discover where their bones were located. The home stood in one and a half acres of woodland, with a small hut only a short walk from the house where Dahmer began collecting large insects and the skeletons of small animals, such as chipmunks and squirrels. Some of these remains were preserved in jars of formaldehyde and stowed or stored within the hut.

Two years later, during a chicken dinner Dahmer asked his father Lionel what would happen if chicken bones were placed in bleach. Lionel pleased by what he believed to be his son's scientific curiosity, demonstrated how to safely bleach and preserve animal bones. Dahmer incorporated these persevering techniques into his bone collecting. He also began collecting dead animals -- including roadkill --- which he would dissect and bury beside the hut, with the skulls occasionally placed atop makeshift crosses.

According to one friend, Dahmer explained to him that he was curious as to how animals "fit together." In one instance in 1975, Dahmer decapitated the carcass of a dog before nailing the body to a tree and impaling the skull or to fix the skull on top of a sharp stake or stick in the woodland behind his house. As a "prank" he later invited a friend to view his display, claiming he had discovered the remains by chance. The same year Dahmer's father Lionel taught his son how to preserve animal bones. Joyce Dahmer his mother began increasing her daily consumption of "Equanil" and "laxatives" and "sleeping pills", further minimizing her tangible contact with her husband and children. Here the raising of a child is important because attention and discipline is of paramount importance in how a child is raised here. The negligence and the calamities and contentions of a father and mother was the possible result and reason that Jeffrey Dahmer went down a path of destruction in his life. And destroyed others who happen to cross his path in life that were the subject of his evil devices perpetrated against these innocent people. Here the lack of chastisement by a father and mother who displayed negligence here that spawned these calamities and contentions that raised a monster in the midst of their lives and other lives; where if they dealt with their son at an early age where there was hope according to Proverbs 19: 13, 18. That instead this downfall of discipline that bound their son Jeffrey Dahmer to foolish and dangerous and evil behaviour that would have not taken place; had they been more cautious about raising him in his very early years. And being more cautious by banning his presence from these surroundings by what he had witnessed regarding seeing those animal bones being removed by his father from beneath the family home while he was growing up from a very young child to his later years according to Proverbs 22: 15.

From his freshman year at Revere High School, Dahmer was seen as an outcast. By age 14, he had begun drinking beer and hard alcohol in the daylight hours, frequently concealing his liquor inside the jacket he wore to school. Dahmer mentioned to one classmate inquired why he was drinking Scotch in a morning history class that the alcohol he consumed was my " medicine." Although largely uncommunicative, in his freshman year Dahmer was seen by staff as polite and highly intelligent but with average grades. He was a competitive tennis player and played briefly in the high school band.

When Dahmer reached puberty, he discovered he was gay, he did not tell his parents. In his early teens had a relationship with anther teenage boy although they never had intercourse. By Dahmer's admission, he began fantasizing about dominating and controlling a completely submissive male partner in his early to mid-teens, and his masturbatory fantasies gradually evolved to his focusing on chests and torsos. these fantasies gradually became intertwined with dissection. When he was about 16 Dahmer conceived a fantasy of render unconscious a particular male jogging, he found attractive, and then making sexual use of his body. On one occasion, Dahmer concealed himself in bushes with a baseball bat to lie in wait for this man. However, the jogger did not pass by on that particular day. Dahmer later admitted this was his first attempt to attack and render an individual submissive to him.

Dahmer was seen by his high school peers as a class clown who often staged pranks which became known as "Doing a Dahmer," these included bleating and simulating "epileptic seizures" or "cerebral palsy" at school and local stores. Occasionally, Dahmer would perform these antics for money to purchase alcohol.

By 1977, Dahmer's grades had declined. His parents hired a private tutor, with limited success. the same year, in an attempt to save their marriage, his parents attended counselling sessions. They continued to quarrel frequently. When Lionel discovered Joyce had engaged in a brief affair in September 1977, they decided to divorce, telling their sons they wished to do so amicably. The process of their divorce soon became increasingly bitter and acrimonious or with harsh language and Lionel moved out of the house in early 1978, temporarily residing in a motel on North Cleveland Massillon Road.

In May 1978 Dahmer graduated from high school. A few weeks before his graduation, one of his teachers observed Dahmer sitting close to the school parking lot, drinking several cans of beer. When the teacher threatened to report the matter, Dahmer informed him he was experiencing "a lot of problems" at home and that the school's guidance counselor was aware of them. That spring, Joyce - contrary to a court order and without informing Lionel --- she moved out of the family home with Jeffrey Dahmer's younger brother David to live with relatives in Chippewa Falls, Wisconsin. Dahmer had just turned 18 and remained in the family home. Dahmer's parents' divorce was finalized on July 24, 1978. Joyce was awarded custody of her younger son David and alimony payments.

Dahmer committed his first murder in 1978, three weeks after his graduation. On June 18, Dahmer picked up a hitchhiker named Steven Mark Hicks, who was almost 19. Dahmer lured Hicks to his house on the pretext or to conceal his real intentions by offering up front to drink with Hicks. Hicks, who had been hitchhiking to a rock concert at Chippewa Lake Park, Ohio agreed to accompany Dahmer to his house upon the promise of "a few beers" with Dahmer; as he had the house to himself. According to Dahmer, the sight of the bare-chested Hicks standing at the roadside stirred his sexual feelings, although when Hicks began talking about girls, he knew any sexual passes he made would be rebuffed or be rejected or criticized sharply. After several hours of talking, drinking and listening to music. Hicks wanted to leave but Dahmer didn't want him to leave. Dahmer bludgeoned Hicks with a 10-pound (4.5 kg) dumbbell. He later stated that he struck Hicks twice from behind with the dumbbell as Hicks sat upon a chair. When Hicks fell unconscious, Dahmer strangled him to death with the bar of the dumbbell, then stripped the clothes from Hicks' body before exploring his chest with his hands, then masturbating as he stood above the corpse. Hours later Dahmer dragged the body to the basement.

The following day, Dahmer dissected Hicks' body in his basement. He later buried the remains in a shallow grave in his back yard. Several weeks later, he unearthed the remains and pared the flesh from the bones or trim the flesh from the bones and for the flesh on the bones to be dissolved in acid before flushing the solution down toilet. He crushed the bones with a sledgehammer and scattered them in the woodland behind the family home. Six weeks after the murder of Hicks, Dahmer's father and his fiancée returned to his home, where they discovered Dahmer living alone. That August, Dahmer enrolled at "Ohio State University (OSU), hoping to major in business. Dahmer's sole term at OSU was completely unproductive, largely because of persistent alcohol abuse. He received failing grades in "Introduction to Anthropology," "Classical Civilizations," and "Administrative Science." The only course Dahmer was successful at was " Riflery " or the practice of shooting at targets with a rifle; where here he received a B- grade. His overall average of all grades or Grade point average (GPA) was 0.45/4.0. On occasion, Lionel paid a surprise visit to visit to his son, only to find his room strewn with empty liquor bottles. Despite his father having paid in advance for the second term, Dahmer dropped out of OSU after just three months.

In January 1979, on his father's urging, Dahmer enlisted in the "United States Army." He underwent basic training at "Fort McClellan in Anniston, Alabama" before training as a medical specialist at "Fort Sam Houston in San Antonio Texas." He was occasionally reprimanded for intoxication while stationed at "Fort Sam Houston." On one occasion, an instance of insubordination resulted in his entire platoon being punished, earning Dahmer a severe beating from his fellow recruits.

On July 13th / 1979, Dahmer was deployed to " Baumholder, West Germany," where he served as a "combat medic in 2nd Battalion, 68th Armored Regiment, 8th Infantry Division." According to published reports, in Dahmer's first year of service, he was an average or slightly above average soldier. Owing to Dahmer's alcohol abuse, his performance deteriorated and in March 1981, he was deemed unsuitable for military service and was later discharged from the army. He received an " honorable discharge," as his superiors did not believe that any problems Dahmer had in the army would be applicable to civilian life.

On March 24th / 1981, Dahmer was sent to "Fort Jackson, South Carolina," for debriefing and provided with a plane ticket to travel anywhere in the country. Dahmer later told police he felt he could not return home to face his father, so he opted to travel to "Miami Beach Florida," both because he was "tired of the cold" and an attempt to live by his own means. In Florida Dahmer found a job at a delicatessen and rented a room in a nearby motel. He spent most of his salary on alcohol and was soon evicted from the motel for non-payment. Dahmer initially spent his evenings on the beach as he continued to work at the sandwich shop until phoning his father and asking to return to Ohio in September of the same year.

After his return to Ohio, Dahmer initially lived with his father and stepmother and insisted on being delegated numerous chores to occupy his time while he looked for work. He continued to drink heavily, and two weeks after his return, he was arrested for "drunk and disorderly conduct." He was fined 60 dollars and given a "suspended 10-day sentence." Dahmer's father tried unsuccessfully to wean his son off alcohol. In December 1981, he and Dahmer's stepmother sent him to live with his grandmother in "West Allis, Wisconsin." Dahmer's grandmother was the only family member to whom Dahmer displayed any affection. they hoped that her influence, plus the change of location, might persuade Dahmer to quit drinking, find a job, and live responsibly.

Initially, Dahmer's living arrangements with his grandmother were harmonious: he accompanied her to church, willingly undertook chores, actively sought work and abided by most of her house rules although he continued to drink and smoke. In early 1982, he found employment as a "phlebotomist" or a medical nurse who draws blood from patients for the purpose of screening or examination of a patient's medical condition or for toxicology purposes at the Milwaukee Blood Plasma Center. He held this job for a total of ten months before being laid off. Dahmer remained unemployed for over two years, during which he lived upon whatever money his grandmother gave him.

Shortly before losing his job, Dahmer was arrested for "indecent exposure." On August 8th / 1982, at "Wisconsin State Fair Park," he was observed exposing himself "on the south side of the Coliseum in which 25 people were present including women and children." For this incident, he was convicted and fined 50 dollars plus court costs.

In January 1985, Dahmer was hired as a mixer at the "Milwaukee Ambrosia Chocolate Factory," where he worked from 11 p.m. to 7 a.m. six nights per week, with Saturday evenings off. Shortly after he found this job, an incident occurred in which Dahmer was propositioned by another man while reading in the " West Allis Public Library. The stranger threw Dahmer a note offering to perform " fellatio " upon him. Although Dahmer did not respond to this proposition, the incident stirred in his mind the fantasies of control and dominance he had developed as a teenager, and he began to familiarize himself with Milwaukee's gay bars, "gay bathhouses," and bookstores. He also stole a male mannequin from a store, which he briefly used for "sexual stimulation," until his grandmother discovered the item stowed in a closet and demanded he discard it.

By 1985, Dahmer had begun to regularly frequent the bathhouses, which he later described as being "relaxing places," but during his sexual encounters, he became frustrated at his partners' moving during the act. Following his arrest, he stated: "I trained myself to view people as objects of pleasure instead of as people." For this reason, beginning in June 1986, he administered sleeping pills to his partners, giving them liquor laced with sedatives. He then waited for his partner to fall asleep before performing various sexual acts. To maintain an adequate supply of this medication, Dahmer informed doctors he worked nights and required the tablets to adjust to that schedule.

 After approximately 12 such instances, the bathhouses' administration revoked Dahmer's membership, and he began to use hotel rooms to continue this practice that has no respect towards a man or no affection towards a female or any human being for that matter; and so in the last days we witness this " Ancient Blood of Violence " today; that has happened more frequently in these last days just before the return of Christ; and how here Dahmer was a lover of pleasures more than a lover of God and being a traitor and a despiser of those that are good and being unthankful and disobedient and unholy towards his parents according to 2nd Timothy 3: 1, 2, 3, 4.

Shortly after his bathhouse memberships were revoked, Dahmer read a report in a newspaper regarding the upcoming funeral of an 18-year-old male. He conceived the idea of stealing the freshly interred corpse or deposited dead body in a coffin or in the earth. According to Dahmer he attempted to dig up the coffin from the ground, but found the soil too hard and abandoned the plan. Here a dead body or corpse is not to be even touched by a born again Christian that is born again by blood and water let alone to be handled as a mannequin for sexual gratification since being defiled by a corpse is a total violation against God and of God's holiness and that a soul that touches a dead body is unclean for 7 days where he or she should not eat any food for 7 days. If you fail to purify yourself or which refers to fast for 7 days and shower with water after fasting 7 days you could die or be "cut off" by God since the term "cut off" means also to end one's life. This only applies to someone born again by the blood and water of Christ according to the New Testament. And in the Old Testament period of ancient times it meant to be cut off or die a death by God; or you would be "cut off" by God if you were a believer of God if you touched a dead body according to Numbers 19: 11, 12, 13, 14, 15, 16, 17, 18, 19, 20, 21, 22. But infidels like Dahmer would be not effected or be subject to death by touching or severely handling a dead body or corpse from a grave.

On September 8th / 1986, Dahmer was arrested upon a charge of lewd and lascivious behaviour for masturbating in the presence of two 12-year-old boys as he stood close to the Kinnikinic River. He initially claimed he had merely been urinating, unaware that there were witnesses, but soon admitted the offense. The charge was changed to disorderly conduct and, on March 10, 1987, Dahmer was sentenced to one year of probation, with additional instructions to undergo counselling. Here a score of these sins of Dahmer are such things that will not inherit the kingdom of God for any of us who commit sins as severe as what Dahmer has committed here in his long rampage of sins as mentioned in this detailed story of him according to Galatians 5: 19, 20, 21.

On November 20, 1987 Dahmer, at the time residing with his grandmother in West Allis, encountered a 25-year-old man from Ontonagon Michigan, named Steven Tuomi at a bar and persuaded him to return to the Ambassador Hotel in Milwaukee, where Dahmer had rented a room for the evening. According to Dahmer, he had no intention of killing Tuomi, but intended to simply drug him and lie beside him as he explored his body.

The following morning, Dahmer awoke to find Tuomi lying beneath him on the bed, his chest "crushed in" and "black and blue" with bruises. Blood was seeping from the corner of his mouth, and Dahmer's fists and one forearm were extensively bruised. Dahmer later said he had no memory of having killed Tuomi, and that he "could not believe this happened."

Dahmer purchased a large suitcase, in which he transported Tuomi's body to his grandmother's residence. One week later, he severed the head, arms, and legs, then filleted the bones from his body before cutting the flesh into pieces small enough to handle. Dahmer placed the flesh inside plastic garbage bags. He wrapped the bones inside a sheet and pounded them into splinters with a sledgehammer. The dismemberment process took Dahmer approximately two hours. He disposed of all of Tuomi's remains, excluding the head, in the trash.

For two weeks following Tuomi's killing, Dahmer retained Tuomi's head wrapped in a blanket. After two weeks, Dahmer boiled the head in a mixture of Soilax (An alkali-based industrial detergent) and bleach in an effort to retain the skull, which he then used as stimulus for masturbation. Eventually, the skull became too brittle by this bleaching process, so Dahmer pulverized the skull and disposed of it. According to Dahmer, Tuomi's murder was a pivotal incident after which he did not try to control his compulsions. He began to actively seek victims with varied tranquilizers such as triazolam or temazepam before shortly after engaging in sexual activity with them. Once his victim was unconscious, he strangled them to death.

Two months after the Tuomi killing, Dahmer encountered a 14- year-old Native American prostitute, James Doxtator. Dahmer lured him to his grandmother's residence with an offer of 50 dollars to pose for nude pictures. They engaged in sexual activity before Dahmer drugged Doxtator and strangled him on the floor of the cellar. Dahmer left the body in the cellar for one week before dismembering it much in the same manner as he had done with Tuomi's body. He placed all of Doxtator's remains (excluding the skull) in the trash. The skull was boiled and cleansed in bleach before Dahmer found that it, too, had been rendered brittle by the process. He pulverized the skull two weeks later.

On March 24th / 1988, Dahmer met a 22-year-old bisexual man, Richard Guerrero, outside a gay bar called the "Phoenix." Dahmer lured Guerrero to his grandmother's residence offering him 50 dollars to spend the night with him. He drugged Guerrero with sleeping pills, strangled him with a leather strap and fellated the corpse. Dahmer dismembered Guerrero's body within 24 hours, again disposing of the remains in the trash and retaining the skull before pulverizing it several months later.

On April 23 /1988 Dahmer lured Ronald Flowers Jr. to his house; however, after giving Flowers a drugged coffee, both he and Flowers heard Dahmer's grandmother call, "Is that you, Jeff?" Although Dahmer replied in a manner that led his grandmother to believe he was alone, she observed that he was not alone. Because of this, Dahmer was unable to kill Flowers, instead waiting until Flowers had become unconscious before taking him to the county General Hospital.

In September 1988, Dahmer's grandmother asked him to move out, largely because of his drinking, and his habit of bringing young men to her house late at night and the foul smells emanating from the basement and the garage ---was it the strong foul odors of perverted sex and the strong odor of dead corpses that went through this basement and garage? Dahmer found a one-bedroom apartment at 808 North 24th Street and moved into his new residence on September 25th. Two days later, he was arrested for drugging and sexually fondling a 13-year-old boy whom he had lured to his home on a false offering to pose for photographs to instead to drug him and have sex with him or by the pretext of posing nude for photographs.

Dahmer's father hired an attorney named Gerald Boyle to defend his son. At Boyle's request, Dahmer's underwent a series of "psychological evaluations" prior to his court hearings. The evaluations found that Dahmer harbored deep feelings of alienation. A second evaluation two months later revealed Dahmer to be an impulsive individual, suspicious of others, and dismayed by his lack of accomplishments in life. His probation officer also referenced a 1987 diagnosis of Dahmer suffering from a "schizoid personality disorder" for presentation to the court.

On January 30th / 1989, Dahmer pleaded guilty to the charges of second-degree sexual assault and of enticing a child for immoral purposes.

Sentencing was suspended until May. On March 20th, Dahmer commenced a ten-day Easter absence from work, during which he moved back into his grandmother's home.

Two months after his conviction and two months prior to his sentencing, Dahmer murdered his fifth victim, a 24-year-old mixed-race aspiring model, Anthony Sears, whom he met at a gay bar on March 25th / 1989. According to Dahmer, on this particular occasion he was not looking to commit a crime, however, shortly before closing time that evening, Sears "just started to talk to me" Dahmer says ---- here Dahmer lured Sears to his grandmother's home, where the pair engaged in oral sex before Dahmer drugged and strangled Sears. The following morning, Dahmer placed the corpse in his grandmother's bathtub, where he decapitated the body before attempting to flay or skin the corpse that flaying here refers to peeling the skin off the corpse by keeping the skin after it is removed intact as a whole section or portion. He stripped the flesh from the body, pulverized the bones, which he disposed of in the trash. According to Dahmer, he found Sears "exceptionally attractive," and Sears was the first victim from whom he permanently retained any body parts: he preserved Sears' head and Genitalia in acetone and stored them in a wooden box, which he later placed in his work locker. When he moved to a new address the following year, he took the remains there.

On May 23rd / 1989, Dahmer was sentenced to five years of probation and one year in the House of Correction, with work release permitted so he could keep his job. He was also required to register as a sex offender. Two months before his scheduled release Dahmer was paroled from his regimen. His five years of probation imposed in 1989 began at this point. Dahmer temporarily moved back to his grandmother's home in West Allis. On May 14th / 1990 Dahmer moved out of his grandmother's house and into 924 North 25th Street, Apartment 213, taking Sears mummified head and genitals with him. Although located in a high crime area, Dahmer's new apartment was close to his workplace, was furnished, and at 300 dollars per month inclusive of all bills excluding electricity, which was economical. Within one week of him moving to this address, Dahmer killed his sixth victim, Raymond Smith. Smith was a 32-year-old prostitute whom Dahmer lured to his apartment with the promise of 50 dollars for sex. Inside the apartment, he gave Smith a drink laced with seven sleeping pills, then manually strangled him.

The following day, Dahmer purchased a polaroid camera, with which he took several pictures of Smith's body in suggestive positions before dismembering him in the bathroom. He boiled the legs, arms and pelvis in a steel kettle with Soilax, which allowed him to rinse the bones in his sink. Dahmer dissolved the remainder of Smith's skeleton --- excluding the skull --- in a container filled with acid. He later spray-painted Smith's skull, which he placed alongside the skull of Sears upon a black towel inside a filing cabinet.

Approximately one week after the murder of Smith, on or about May 27th, Dahmer lured another young man to his apartment. On this occasion, Dahmer accidently consumed the drink laden with sedatives intended for his guest. When he awoke the following day, he discovered the man had stolen several items of clothing and 300 dollars and a watch. Dahmer never reported this incident to the police although on May 29th, he divulged to his probation officer that he had been robbed.

In June 1990 Dahmer lured a 27-year-old acquaintance, Edward Smith, to his apartment, where he drugged and strangled him. On this occasion, rather than immediately acidifying the skeleton or repeatedly doing the previous processes of bleaching which had rendered previous victims' skulls brittle, Dahmer placed Smiths skeleton in his freezer for several months in the hope it would not retain moisture. Freezing the skeleton did not remove moisture, and the skeleton of this victim was acidified several months later. Dahmer accidently destroyed the skull when he placed it in the oven to dry --- a process that caused the skull to explode. Dahmer later informed police that he had felt "rotten" about Smith's murder, as he had been unable to retain any body parts of his body. Here Dahmer's statement was as follows: "It was my way of remembering their appearance, their physical beauty. I also wanted to keep... if I couldn't keep them with me whole, I at least could keep their skeletons." Here Jeffrey Dahmer, recollecting his motivations for both photographing his victims and retaining sections of their skeletal structure. ----- February / 1993.

Less than three months after the murder of Edward Smith, Dahmer encountered a 22-year-old Chicago native named Ernest Miller outside a bookstore on the corner of North 27th Street. Miller agreed to accompany Dahmer to his apartment for 50 dollars and further agreed to allow him to listen to his heart and stomach. When Dahmer attempted to perform oral sex upon Miller, he was informed, "That'll cost you extra", whereupon Dahmer gave Miller a drink laced with two sleeping pills. On this occasion, Dahmer had only two sleeping pills to give his victim. Therefore, he killed Miller by slashing his carotid artery where on each side of the neck here consists of a carotid artery on each side. He used the same knife that he used to dissect his victims' bodies. Miller Bled to death within minutes. Dahmer then posed the nude body for various suggestive Polaroid photographs before placing the body in his bathtub for dismemberment. Dahmer repeatedly kissed and talked to the severed head while he dismembered the remainder of the body.

Dahmer wrapped Miller's heart, liver, biceps, and portions of flesh from the legs in plastic bags and placed them in the freezer for later consumption. He boiled the remaining flesh and organs into a "jelly-like substance" using Soilax, which enabled him to rinse the flesh off the skeleton, which he intended to retain. To preserve the skeleton, Dahmer placed the bones in a light bleach solution for 24 hours before allowing them to dry upon a cloth for one week. The severed head initially placed in the refrigerator before being stripped of flesh, then painted and coated with enamel.

Three weeks after the murder Miller, on September 24th / 1990 Dahmer encountered a 22-year-old father of two named David Thomas at the "Grand Avenue Mall" that spans three city blocks in the downtown neighbourhood of Westtown in Milwaukee, Wisconsin. He persuaded David Thomas to return to his apartment for a few drinks, with additional money on offer if he would pose for photographs. In his statement to police after his arrest, Dahmer said that, after giving Thomas a drink Laden with sedatives, he did not feel attracted to him, but was afraid to allow to awaken, fearing that he would be angry over having been drugged. Therefore, he strangled him and dismembered the body --- intentionally retaining no body parts whatsoever. He photographed the dismemberment process and retained these photographs, which later aided in Thomas's identification.

Following the murder of Thomas, Dahmer did not kill anyone for almost 5 months although on a minimum of five occasions between October 1990 and February 1991, he unsuccessfully attempted to lure men to his apartment. He regularly complained of feelings of both anxiety and depression to his probation officer throughout 1990, with frequent references to his sexuality, his solitary lifestyle., financial difficulties, and --- shortly before "Thanksgiving" -- his apprehension regarding meeting and facing his father and his younger brother. On several occasions, Dahmer also referred to harboring suicidal thoughts.

In February 1991, Dahmer observed a 17-year-old named Curtis Straughter standing at a bus stop near "Marquette University." According to Dahmer, he lured Straughter into his apartment with an offer of money for posing for nude photos, with added incentive of sexual intercourse. Dahmer drugged Straughter, cuffed his hands behind his back, then strangled him to death with a leather strap. He then dismembered Straughter, retaining his skull, hands, and genitals and photographing each stage of the dismemberment process.

Less than two months later, on April 7th, Dahmer encountered a 19-year-old named Errol Lindsey walking to get a key cut. Dahmer lured Lindsey to his apartment where he drugged him, then drilled a hole in his skull through which he injected "hydrochloric acid " with a baster or to moisten. According to Dahmer, Lindsey awoke after this experiment; which Dahmer had conceived in the hope of inducing a permanent, unresistant, submissive state. Here Lindsey awoke saying: "I have a headache. What time is it?" In response to this, Dahmer again drugged Lindsey, then strangled him. He decapitated Lindsey and retained his skull. He then flayed Lindsey's body placing the skin in a solution of cold water and salt for several weeks in the hope of permanently retaining it. Reluctantly, he disposed of Lindsey's skin when he noted it had become too frayed and brittle.

By 1991, fellow residents of the Oxford Apartments had repeatedly complained to the building's manager, Sopa Princewill of the foul smells emanating from Apartment 213, in addition to the sounds of falling objects and the occasional sound of a chainsaw. Princewill contacted Dahmer in response to these complaints on several occasions, although he initially excused the odors emanating from his apartment as being caused by his freezer breaking, causing the contents to become "spoiled." On later occasions, he informed Princewill that the reason for the resurgence of the order was that several of his tropical fish had recently died, and that he would take care of the matter.

On May 24th / 1991, Dahmer encountered 31-year-old aspiring model Tony Hughes at a nightclub. He was lured to Dahmer's apartment with an offer of Dahmer injected hydrochloric acid into his skull in an effort to disable his "wil " and render him submissive, although on this occasion, the drilling and injection proved fatal.

On the afternoon of May 26th / 1991, Dahmer encountered a 14-year-old Lao teenager, Konerak Sinthasomphone on "Wisconsin Avenue." Unknown to Dahmer, Sinthasomphone was the younger brother of the boy he had molested in 1988. Dahmer offered Sinthasomphone money to accompany him to his apartment to pose for Polaroid pictures. According to Dahmer, Sinthasomphone was initially reluctant to the proposal, before changing his mind and accompanying him to his apartment, where he posed for two pictures in his underwear before Dahmer drugged him into unconsciousness and performed oral sex on him. Before Sinthasomphone fell unconscious, Dahmer led the boy into his bedroom, where the body of Tony Hughes, whom Dahmer had killed three days earlier, lay naked on the floor. According to Dahmer, he " believed that Sinthasomphone saw this body " yet did not react to seeing the bloated corpse --- likely because of the effects of the sleeping pills that Sinthasomphone had ingested.

On this occasion, Dahmer drilled a single narrow hole into the crown of Sinthasomphone's skull, through which he injected hydrochloric acid into the frontal lobe. Dahmer then drank several beers while lying alongside Sinthasomphone before briefly falling asleep, then leaving his apartment to drink at a bar and purchase more alcohol.

In the early morning hours of May 27th / 1991 Dahmer returned toward his apartment to discover Sinthasomphone sitting naked on the corner of 25th and State, talking in "Lao" language, with three distressed young women standing near him. Dahmer approached the women and told them that Sinthasomphone whom he referred to by the alias "John Hmong," was his friend, and attempted to lead him to his apartment by the arm. The three women dissuaded Dahmer, explaining they had phoned 911.

Upon the arrival of two Milwaukee police officers, John Balcerzak and Joseph Gabrish, Dahmer's demeanor relaxed; and here he told the officers that Sinthasomphone was his 19-year-old boyfriend, that he had drunk too much following a quarrel, and that he frequently behaved in this manner when intoxicated. Dahmer added his lover had consumed Jack Daniel's whisky that evening.

The three women were exasperated or annoyed or even to the point of being angry when one of the trio attempted to indicate to one of the officers who both officers had observed no injuries beyond a scrape to Sinthasomphone's knee and believed him to be intoxicated --- and that Sinthasomphone had blood upon his testicles, and was bleeding from his rectum and that he had seemingly struggled against Dahmer's attempts to walk him to his apartment prior to their arrival, the officer harshly informed her to "butt out," and "shut the hell up" and to not interfere.

Shortly after the arrival of the "Milwaukee" police officers, three members of the "Milwaukee Fire Department" arrived at the scene. these individuals also examined Sinthasomphone for injuries and provided a yellow blanket for the police to cover Sinthasomphone. One of the three believed Sinthasomphone needed treatment, but the police officers directed the fire department personal to leave. Shortly thereafter, officer Richard Porubcan arrived at the scene. He and officer Gabrish followed by officer Balcerzak escorted Dahmer and Sinthasomphone to Dahmer's apartment as Dahmer repeatedly commented on the general crime in the neighborhood and of his appreciation of the police.

Inside his apartment and in an effort to verify his claim that he and Sinthasomphone were lovers. Dahmer showed the officers the two semi-nude Polaroid pictures he had taken of Sinthasomphone the previous evening. Though Balcerzak said he smelled nothing unusual, Gabrish later stated he noted a strange scent reminiscent of excrement inside the apartment. This odor emanated from the decomposing body of Tony Hughes. Dahmer stated to investigate this odor, one officer simply "peeked his head around the bedroom, but really didn't take a good look." The officers then left, with a departing remark that Dahmer "take good care" of

Sinthasomphone. This incident was listed by the officers as a domestic dispute. Here Dahmer used reverse psychology to deceive the officers by saying that they should investigate this "odor" knowing full well that Tony Hughes's body was in the bedroom and that Dahmer knew that he would not be under suspicion by the officers after asking the officers to quote "check the apartment for odors" to which the officers were deceived into believing that Dahmer had nothing to hide because of Dahmer making such a statement of this sort. Here this is what we have, that is called "fair speech" given all along by Dahmer to deceive the police officers and also all along in this so-called incident listed by the police officers as a "domestic dispute" according to Proverbs 26: 25.

Upon the departure of the three police officers from his apartment, Dahmer again injected hydrochloric acid into Sinthasomphone's brain. This second injection proved fatal. The following day on May 28th / 1991 Dahmer took a day's leave from work to devote himself to the dismemberment of the bodies of Sinthasomphone and Hughes. He retained both victim's skulls.

On June 30th / 1991 Dahmer traveled to Chicago, where he encountered a 20-year-old named Matt Turner at a bus station. Turner accepted Dahmer's offer to travel to Milwaukee for a "professional photo shoot." At the apartment, Dahmer drugged, strangled and dismembered Turner and placed his head and internal organs in separate plastic bags in the freezer. Turner was not reported missing. Five days later, on July 5th, Dahmer lured 23-year-old Jeremiah Weinberger from a Chicago bar to his apartment on the promise of spending the weekend with him. He drugged Weinberger and twice injected boiling water through his skull, sending him into a coma from which he died two days later.

On July 15th / 1991 Dahmer encountered 24-year-old Oliver Lacy at the corner of 27th and Kilbourn. Lacy agreed to Dahmer's ruse or of trickery of convincing him to posing nude for photographs and accompanied him to his apartment, where the pair engaged in tentative sexual activity before Dahmer drugged Lacy. On this occasion, Dahmer intended to prolong the time he spent with Lacy while alive. After unsuccessfully attempting to render Lacy unconscious with "chloroform" which is a powerful anesthetic, he phoned his workplace to request a day's absence, this was granted, although the next day, he was suspended.

After strangling Lacy, Dahmer had sex with the corpse before dismembering him. He placed Lacy's head and heart in the refrigerator and his skeleton in the freezer. Four days later, on July 19th, Dahmer received word that he was dismissed. Upon receipt of this news, Dahmer lured 25-year-old Joseph Bradehoft to his apartment. Bradehoft was strangled and left lying on Dahmer's bed covered with a sheet for two days. On July 21st, Dahmer removed the sheet to find the head covered in maggots. He decapitated the body, cleaned the head and placed it in the refrigerator. He later acidified Bradehoft's torso, along with those of two other victims killed the previous month who were Oliver Lacy and Matt Turner.

On July 22nd / 1991 Dahmer approached three men with an offer of 100 dollars to accompany him to his apartment to pose for nude photographs, drink beer and simply keep company. One of the trios, 32-year-old Tracy Edwards, agreed to accompany him to his apartment. Upon entering Dahmer's apartment, Edwards noted a foul odor and several boxes of Hydrochloric acid on the floor, which Dahmer claimed to use for cleaning bricks. After some minor conversation, Edwards responded to Dahmer's request to turn his head and view the tropical fish, whereupon Dahmer placed a handcuff upon his wrist. When Edwards asked, "What's happening?" Dahmer unsuccessfully attempted to cuff his wrists together, then told Edwards to accompany him to the bedroom to pose for nude pictures. While inside the bedroom, Edwards noted nude male posters on the wall and that a videotape of "The Exorcist III" was playing. He also noted a blue 57-gallon drum in the corner, from which a strong odor emanated.

Dahmer then brandished a knife and informed Edwards he intended to take nude pictures of him. In an attempt to appease Dahmer; Edwards unbuttoned his shirt, saying he would allow him to do so if he would remove the handcuffs and put the knife away. In response to this promise, Dahmer simply turned his attention towards the TV. Edwards observed Dahmer rocking back and forth and chanting before turning his attention back to him. He placed his head on Edwards chest, listened to his heartbeat and, with the knife pressed against his intended victim, and informed Edwards he intended to eat his heart.

In continuous attempts to prevent Dahmer from attacking him, Edwards repeated that he was Dahmer's friend and that he was not going to run away. Edwards had decided he was going to either jump from a window or run through the unlocked locked front door upon the next available opportunity. When Edwards next, stated he needed to use the bathroom, he asked if could sit with a beer in the living room, where there was air conditioning. Dahmer consented, and the pair walked to the living room when Edwards exited the bathroom. Inside the living room, Edwards waited until he observed Dahmer have a momentary lapse of concentration before requesting to use the bathroom again. When Edwards rose from the couch, he noted Dahmer was not holding the handcuffs, whereupon Edwards punched him in the face, knocking Dahmer off balance and ran out the front door.

At 11: 30 p.m. on July 22nd / 1991 Edwards flagged down tow Milwaukee police officers, Robert Rauth and Rolf Mueller, at the corner of North 25th Street. The officers noted Edwards had a handcuff attached to his wrist, whereupon he explained to the officers that a "freak" had placed the handcuffs upon him and asked if the police could remove them. When the officers' handcuff keys failed to fit the brand of handcuffs, Edwards agreed to accompany the officers to the apartment where, Edwards stated, he had spent the previous five hours before escaping.

When the officers and Edwards arrived at Apartment 213, Dahmer invited the trio inside and acknowledged he had placed the handcuffs upon Edwards, although he offered no explanation as to why he had done so. At this point, Edwards divulged to the officers that Dahmer had also brandished a large knife upon him and that this had happened in the Bedroom. Dahmer made no comment to this revelation, indicating to one of the officers, Meuller, that the key to the handcuffs was in his bedside dresser. As Mueller entered the bedroom, Dahmer attempted to pass Mueller to retrieve the key himself, whereupon the second officer present, Rauth informed him to "back off."

In the bedroom, Mueller noted there was a large knife beneath the bed. He saw an open drawer which, upon closer inspection, contained scores of Polaroid pictures --- many of which were of human bodies in various stages of dismemberment. Mueller noted decor indicated they had been taken in the same apartment in which they were standing. Mueller walked into the living room to show them to his partner, uttering the words, "These are for real."

When Dahmer saw that Mueller was holding several of his Polaroids, he fought with the officers in an effort to resist arrest. The officers quickly overpowered him, cuffed his hands behind his back, and called a second squad car for back-up. At this point Mueller opened the refrigerator to reveal the freshly severed head of a black male on the bottom shelf. As Dahmer lay pinned on the floor beneath Rauth, he turned his head towards the officers and muttered the words "For what I did I should be dead."

A more detailed search of the apartment, conducted by the Milwaukee police's Criminal Investigation Bureau, revealed a total of four severed heads in Dahmer's kitchen. A total of seven skulls --- some painted, some bleached --- were found in Dahmer's bedroom and inside a closet. Investigators discovered collected blood drippings upon a tray at the bottom of Dahmer's refrigerator, plus two human hearts and a portion of arm muscle, each wrapped inside plastic bags upon the shelves. In Dahmer's freezer investigators discovered an entire torso, plus a bag of human organs and flesh stuck to the ice at the bottom.

Elsewhere in Apartment 213, investigators discovered two entire skeletons, a pair of severed hands, two severed and preserved penises, a mummified scalp and, in the 57-gallon drum, there was further dismembered torsos dissolving in the acid solution. A total of 74 Polaroid pictures detailing the dismemberment of Dahmer's victims were found. In reference to the recovery of body parts and artifacts at 924 North 25th Street, the Chief medical examiner later stated " It was more like dismantling someone's museum, than an actual crime scene."

Beginning in the early hours of July 23rd / 1991, Dahmer was questioned by Detective Patrick Kennedy as to the murders he had committed and the evidence found at his apartment. Over the following two weeks, Kennedy and, later Detective Dennis Murphy conducted numerous interviews with Dahmer which, when combined, totaled over 60 hours. Dahmer waived his right to have a lawyer present through his interrogations, adding he wished to confess all as he had "created this horror and it only makes sense I do everything to put an end to it." He readily admitted to having murdered sixteen young men in Wisconsin since 1987, with one further victim --- Steven Hicks -- killed in Ohio in 1978.

Most of Dahmer's victims had been rendered unconscious prior to their murder, although some had died as a result of having acid or boiling water injected into their brain. As he had no memory of the killing of his second victim, Steven Tuomi, he was unsure whether he was unconscious when beaten to death, although he concede it was possible that his viewing the exposed chest of Tuomi while in a drunken stupor may have led him to unsuccessfully attempt to tear Tuomi's heart from his chest. Almost all the murders Dahmer committed after moving into the Oxford Apartments had involved a ritual of posing the victims' bodies in suggestive positions -- typically with the chest thrust outwards --- prior to dismemberment.

Dahmer readily admitted to engaging in necrophilia with several of his victims' bodies, including performing sexual acts with their "viscera" or the internal organs of their bodies in his bathtub. Having noted that much of the blood pooled inside his victims' chest after death, Dahmer first removed their internal organs, then suspended the torso so the blood drained into his bathtub, before dicing any organs he did not wish to retain and paring the flesh from the body. The bones he wished to dispose of were pulverized or acidified with Soilax and bleach solutions used to aid in the preservation of the skeletons and skulls he wished to keep. Dahmer confessed to having consumed the hearts, liver, biceps and portions of thigh of the three victims he had killed at the Oxford Apartments (Raymond Smith, Ernest Miller and Oliver Lacy), and to have retained the flesh and organs of other victims for intended consumption. Typically, Dahmer would tenderize the body parts he intended to consume prior to preparing meals flavored with various condiments.

Referencing his reasons for consuming his victims, Dahmer stated he initially consumed portions of his victims due to " curiosity " before adding: "I suppose in an odd way, it made me feel they were even more a permanent part of me."

Describing the increase in his rate of killing in the two months prior to his arrest, Dahmer stated he had been "completely swept alon " with his compulsion to kill, adding: "It was an incessant or continual and never-ending desire to be with someone at whatever cost. Someone good looking, really nice looking. It just filled my thoughts all day long." when asked as to why he had preserved a total of seven skulls and the entire skeletons of two victims, Dahmer stated he had been in the process of constructing a private altar of victims' skulls which he had intended to display on the black table located in his living room and upon which he had photographed the bodies of many of his victims.

The display of skulls was to be adorned at each side with the complete skeletons of Miller and Lacy. The four severed heads found in his kitchen were to have all flesh removed and used in this altar, as was the skull of at least one future victim. Incense sticks were to be placed at each end of the black table, above which Dahmer intended to place a large blue lamp with extending blue globe lights. The entire construction was to be placed before a window covered with a black opaque shower curtain, in front of which Dahmer intended to sit in a black leather chair.

When asked in a November 18th / 1991 interview to whom the alter was dedicated, Dahmer replied: "Myself ... it was a place where I could feel at home." He further described his intended altar as a place for meditation, "from where he believed he could draw a sense of power adding: If this (his arrest) had happened six months later, that's what they would have found (which was this constructed altar)." The investigation and interrogation after Dahmer's arrest revealed plans on paper illustrated provided by Dahmer depicting this private altar he had been planning to create or build at the time of his July 1991 arrest.

On July 25th / 1991 Dahmer was charged with four counts of first-degree murder. By August 22nd, he had been charged with a further eleven murders committed in Wisconsin. On September 14th, investigators in Ohio, having uncovered hundreds of bone fragments in woodland behind the address in which Dahmer had confessed to killing his first victim, formally identified two molars and a vertebra with X-ray records of Hicks. Three days later Dahmer was charged by authorities in Ohio with Hick's murder.

Dahmer was not charged with the attempted murder of Edwards, nor with the murder of Tuomi. He was not charged with Tuomi's murder because "Milwaukee County District Attorney" only brought charges where murder could be proven beyond a reasonable doubt and Dahmer had no memory of actually committing this particular murder, for which no physical evidence of the crime existed. At a scheduled preliminary hearing on January 13th / 1992, Dahmer pleaded guilty, but insane to 15 counts of murder.

In Court on February 15th / 1992 Dahmer addressed the court. Dahmer emphasized that he had never desired freedom from following his arrest, and that he "frankly" wished for his own death. He further stressed that none of his murders had been motivated by hatred, that he understood that nothing he either said or did could " undo the terrible harm " he had caused to the families of his victims and the city of Milwaukee, and that he and his doctors believed his criminal behaviour had been motivated by "mental disorders." Dahmer added that this medical knowledge had given him "some peace" and that although he understood that society would never forgive him, he hoped God would. Dahmer closed his statement with: "I know my time in prison will be terrible, but I deserve whatever I get because of what I have done. Thank you, your honor, and I am prepared for your sentence, which I know will be the maximum. I ask for no consideration." He then returned to his seat to await formal sentencing.

Dahmer was then sentenced to life imprisonment plus ten years upon the first two counts. The remaining thirteen counts carried a mandatory sentence of life imprisonment plus seventy years. The death penalty was not an option for Judge Gram to consider at the penalty phase, as Wisconsin had abolished capital punishment in 1853.

Upon sentencing, Dahmer was transferred to the Columbia Correctional Institution. For the first year of his incarceration, Dahmer was placed in solitary confinement due to concerns for his physical safety should he come in contact with fellow inmates. He received ample or generous correspondence from individuals across the world, with several individuals donating money which he spent on items such as cassette recordings, and on stationery or pens and paper and pencils and erasers etc. and cigarettes and magazines.

Upon Dahmer's request, after one year in solitary confinement he was transferred to a less secure unit, where he was assigned a two-hour daily work detail cleaning toilet block. This work detail later expanded to include cleaning the prison gymnasium.

Shortly after completing his lengthy confessions in 1991, Dahmer had requested to detective Murphy that he be given a copy of the Bible. This request was granted and Dahmer gradually devoted himself to Christianity and became a born-again Christian. On his father's urging, he also read creationist books from the institute for Creation Research. In May 1994, Dahmer was baptized by Roy Ratcliff, a minister in the "Church of Christ" and a graduate of "Oklahoma Christian University" whom he had met on April 20. This service was conducted in the prison whirlpool.

Following Dahmer's baptism, Ratcliff visited him on a weekly basis. The two regularly discussed the prospect of death, and Ratcliff later divulged that, in the months prior to his murder, Dahmer had questioned whether he was sinning against God by continuing to live. Referring to his crimes in a 1994 interview with Stone Phillips on Dateline NBC, Dahmer had stated "If a person doesn't think there is a God to be accountable to, then what's the point of trying to modify your behaviour to keep it within acceptable ranges? That's how I thought anyway."

On February 8th / 1992, Fred Fosdal testified on behalf of the prosecution. Fosdal testified to his belief that Dahmer was without mental disease or defect at the time he committed the murders. He described Dahmer as a calculating and cunning individual, able to differentiate between right and wrong, with the ability to control his actions, and whose lust overpowered his morals. Although Fostal did state his belief Dahmer was a paraphiliac, or someone with sexually social unacceptable behaviour such as a pedophile; is that his conclusion was that Dahmer was not a sadist.

I John Bazzanella the author of this book here --- is that I am of the opinion here that Dahmer in my own opinion was indeed extremely cunning and calculating to carry on these mutilations of multiple murders in an apartment where normal people are present and residing in the same resident building he was residing in and for these murders and mutilations to be even carried on for a week without getting caught --- let alone for 14 months in his apartment at 924 North 25th Street Apartment 213 before he was even caught and arrested. Also, this was the most severe cunning and calculating deception of evil that may have occurred in the history of criminological and forensic horrors that transpired from these atrocities and murders of mutilating these victims. And that Dahmer turned his apartment into an anthropological and archaeological museum of horrors. He indeed in his fair speech and handsome appearance was extremely cunning and calculating to deceive these people who were visitors and who were involved with others that were residing in the same apartment building that he was residing in according to Proverbs 26: 25.

The second and final witness to appear for the prosecution, forensic psychiatrist Park Dietz began his testimony on February 12 / 1992 testified that he did not believe Dahmer had any form of mental disease or defect at the time that he committed the crimes, stating that "Dahmer went to great lengths to be alone with his victim and to have no witnesses." He explained that there was ample evidence that Dahmer prepared in advance for each murder, therefore his crimes were not impulsive. Although Dietz did concede any acquisition of a paraphilia was not a matter of personal choice, he stated his belief that Dahmer's habit to becoming intoxicated prior to committing each of the murders was significant, "If he had an impulse to kill or a compulsion to kill," Dietz testified , "he wouldn't have to drink alcohol to overcome it. He only has to drink alcohol to overcome it because he is inhibited against killing.

Following the defense counsel's 75-minute closing argument, Michael McCann delivered his closing argument for the prosecution describing Dahmer as a sane man, in full control of his actions, who simply strove to avoid detection. McCann described Dahmer as a calculating individual who killed to control his victims and retained their bodies " merely to afford" himself prolonged period of sexual pleasure. McCann argued that by pleading guilty but insane to the charges, Dahmer was seeking to escape responsibility for his crimes.

On July 3rd / 1994, a fellow inmate, Osvaldo Durruthy, attempted to slash Dahmer's throat with a razor embedded in a toothbrush as Dahmer sat in the prison chapel after the weekly church service was concluded. Dahmer received superficial wounds and was not seriously hurt in this incident. According to Dahmer's family, he had long been ready to die, and accepted any punishment which might endure in prison. In addition to his father and stepmother maintaining regular contact, Dahmer's mother Joyce also maintained regular contact with her son. Prior to his arrest the two had not seen each other since Christmas 1983. Joyce related that in her weekly phone calls, whenever she expressed concerns for her son's physical well-being. Dahmer responded with comments to the effect of: "It doesn't matter Mom. I don't care if something happens to me."

On the morning of November 28th / 1994, Dahmer left his cell to conduct his assigned work detail. Accompanying him were two fellow inmates, Jesse Anderson and Christopher Scarver. The trio were left unsupervised in the showers of the prison gym for approximately 20 minutes. At approximately 8:10 a.m. Dahmer was discovered on the floor of the bathrooms of the gym suffering from extreme head wounds, he had been severely bludgeoned about the head and face with a 20-inch (51 centimeter) metal bar. His head had also been repeatedly struck against the wall in the assault. Although Dahmer was still alive and was rushed to a nearby hospital, he was pronounced dead one hour later. Anderson had been beaten with the same instrument; he died from his wounds two days later.

Scarver, who was serving a life sentence for a murder committed in 1990, informed authorities he had first attacked Dahmer with the metal bar as Dahmer was cleaning a staff locker room before attacking Anderson as Anderson cleaned an inmate locker room. According to Scarver, Dahmer did not yell or make any noise as he was attacked according to Proverbs 14: 32. Immediately after attacking both men. Scarver who was thought to be schizophrenic, returned to his cell and informed a prison guard: "God told me to do it. Jesse Anderson and Jeffrey Dahmer are dead." Scarver was adamant he had not planned the attacks in advance, although he later divulged to investigators, he had concealed the 20-inch iron bar used to kill both men in his clothing shortly before the killings.

Upon learning of his death, Dahmer's mother Joyce responded angrily to the media: "Now is everybody happy? Now that he's bludgeoned to death, is that good enough for everyone?" The response of the families of Dahmer's victims was mixed: some celebrated the news, while others were saddened. Catherine Lacy, the mother of victim Oliver Lacy, remarked: "The hurt is worse now, because he's not suffering like we are," unquote. Here according to Proverbs 14: 32, 33, 34 is that Scarver persecuted both

Dahmer and Anderson severely by bludgeoning them to death with a metal bar where Jeffrey Dahmer and Jesse Anderson may have made the effort to seek God's forgiveness for their sins. The district attorney who prosecuted Dahmer cautioned against turning Scarver into a folk hero, saying that Dahmer's death was still murder. On May 15th / 1995, Scarver was sentenced to two additional terms of life imprisonment for the murders of Dahmer and Anderson.

Dahmer's handsome appearance and cunning deception could be possibly be deemed as appearing as an angel of light according 2nd Corinthians 11: 13, 14, 15. But may have had a change of mind of his wicked ways according to Ezekiel 33: 11, 12, 13, 14, 15, 16, 17, 18, 19 and Proverbs 14 : 32. Here Dahmer's conscience had invited demons to possess him --- here the thought of having "Thanksgiving" with his family had plagued his conscience with the sickness of the demons he attracted by the spell of his horrific and terrifying crimes of exploring and dismembering severely the human body of his victims and it's organs leaving him with a psychological sickness of severe depression and anxiety; that was brought on by these demons. Here in the beginning of his sins of these crimes that began with his first victim ---these demons were very few in numbers. Giving him that comfort of fulfilling his sexual fantasies by using death as a way to fulfill his lust that he wanted. Not knowing what the end of these sins would be regarding the consequences and the results of the amount of demons that would increase as he went deeper in committing and proceeding further into these crimes of unspeakable and unimaginable horror that caused him to attract a legion of demons to possess him here. And here was also subject of death and wanting to die here that was also his sickness of this psychological terror of anxiety and depression due to the horrific sinful atrocities that he had committed.

 Here it gave him a psychological sickness that may have overwhelmed him to the point that he could possibly no longer carry on with his continual murdering spree that he had committed. Where these murders were coupled with his lust of this severe sexual obsession with death that turned him off by this point in time by his past obsession with Necrophilia here that was brought on by this sickness of severe demonic possession that he brought on to himself by the persistent continuation of these unspeakable horrific crimes. Without rebuking these sins at a very early stage in his life;

that had possibly may have left him open to the lost opportunity of seeking early repentance in order to cast out these demons and be forgiven for these sins and getting rid of these severe psychological burdens of suffering of depression and anxiety that led to suicidal thoughts according to Proverbs 1: 27, 28, 29, 30, 31 and Mark 5: 8, 9 and Matthew 8: 16, 17 and Proverbs 1: 33. Whether this is the case no one knows what the Judgments of God are according to Romans 11: 31, 32, 33. But it is possible that Dahmer's conscience had played on his mind giving him the spirit of repentance truly from the heart spawning that guilt he had after those horrific dismemberments and total desecration and murders of his victims and their corpses that were dissected and dismembered after death. That here he may have had a conscience of remorse so great that he knew and felt he didn't deserve to live where he sought that offer of forgiveness from God in exchange for his life according to Ezekiel 33: 14 and Proverbs 14: 32.

Here this is definitely a case of the "Ancient Blood of Violence" that has been perpetrated by a human being in our day and age in modern history where this type of behaviour and obsession with human blood, flesh, skulls, and bones has the characteristic behaviour of an ancient man of ancient times dating back to the Neanderthal that perpetrated this kind of behaviour on their victims or enemies. That even ancient man has not even possibly done such odd sexual behaviour and perverted sexual obsession like Dahmer has done here unlike the Neanderthal that has done with their own specie let alone to their own related animal species that are like either mammals related to humans such as Apes or Monkeys or Gorillas or a lesser specie like non- human related vertebrates of every other kind of animal or a lesser life form like insects.

I say sarcastically speaking that Dahmer is quite a sick character and that Dahmer possessed the most horrific violent and sexual acts of any person who could even possibly conceive or imagine to perpetrate in the sight of not only mankind but God. Who Dahmer has this mind of evil embedded in him so deep that it would shatter one's own confidence of reality and from everything from multiple government institutions and governmental psychiatric and scientific institutions to one owns 5 senses! Frightening behaviour with the obsession of the death of a human being and its corpse afterwards to be handled and abused in such a despicable way as to desecrate a human being after death this way; is absolutely incomprehensible to the 10th degree of this man named Jeffrey Dahmer. My question is what happened to this man to perpetrate such severely deplorable acts of sexual obsession and obsession with death ---- is want I would love to know like the rest of us who cannot comprehend this outrageous insanity shrouded of not, in some sort of monster, but what we would call a human being as a truly concealed monster, of something that not even Hollywood could imagine in their movies of horror. Yet as we read this story it is an undeniable and unbelievable reality that is conceived by some sort of Satanic force that may have mysteriously possessed Dahmer to commit such insane behaviour that would even re-write the research work and books of psychiatry of the diagnostics of human behaviour and humans who possess this type of inexplicable insanity.

Here a vile person shall be no more be called liberal nor will the morose person or churl person of a capricious and sullen or gloomy disposition said to be bountiful and making empty the soul of the hungry and he will cause the drink of the thirsty to fail. Are these sickening revelations of Dahmer's crimes and sexual perverted offences that has made or caused people to not eat and drink in peace or refuse to eat and drink altogether according to Isaiah 32: 5, 6, 7?

Here we are humans prone to sin and that some get possessed with demons that can cause sin. What is sin? It is a state of the depravity of man and this depravity comes in all forms and different levels of severity in the sickness it possesses in this corrupt nature man possesses in this occurrence we call sin. Sin had originated in the ancient period of Genesis and it was made more severe and extremely deplorable by the Extraterrestrial Sons of God who unlawfully had mated with the daughters of men on this planet according bringing sin to a more despicable level that brought on their offsprings who were deformed offsprings of beings of Giantism and Dwarfism and deformity that also introduced the presence of devil or demonic spirits that gave sin that vehicle of extreme depravity that possessed man's weak will to resist this possession therefore bringing man to a state of immorality so despicable that the human race had in its midst the monsters of crime and criminal and homicidal activity like Dahmer had committed that was so great that it has boggled our human minds. May Dahmer find that peace he was looking for when he offered without a complaint to give up his life. And may we all find that peace as well and that the chapter of violence ends in this world with the coming of our Lord and Saviour Jesus Christ and that this chapter of violence of ours that has gone on since the time of Genesis will eventually come to its end.

Here during this reading and writing of Jeffrey Dahmer's s story I experienced a mild form of Post-Traumatic Stress Disorder where I experienced anxiety and depression that set in because of the disturbing nature of his crime and the description of his crime that was written. Here the cause of this P.T.S.D. was the demons that possessed me where I had to fast for about 24 hours (Matthew 6: 25) and refrain from writing and viewing the written rhetoric of Jeffrey Dahmer's story of these horrific murders he committed. These atrocious crimes of human dismemberment of a corpse had also affected those like paramedics and police officers and fire fighters and military personnel and soldiers of war that subjected some of them to a more severe Post Traumatic Stress Disorder that it eventually drove them to suicide. Thankfully for some of us we did not have to experience that P.T.S.D. and witness this bloodshed and dismemberment of some of these corpses; where you could have been one of these people or personnel I just mentioned here in the military or the police force or paramedic emergency service or the fire department to have been right there witnessing when these atrocities that were; or have taken place and have experienced that Post Traumatic Stress Disorder that drove some to suicide.

Throughout history Man has shown extraordinary imagination in inventing penalties and sentences for crimes committed by fellow man. The Romans in particular had an almost theatrical quality in the way these punishments were doled out. One of the worst was reserved for parricide --- the killing of a parent -- in which the prisoner was placed in a sack with several live animals and thrown into water: known as the "poena cullei" or "penalty of the sack."

The German philosopher Erich Fromm said that we are "The only animal that enjoys doing evil to its own kind without any rational biological or social benefit." But sometimes there was, and still is, a moral pretext: the defense of society. Aristotle himself affirms in his work "Politics" that the most necessary public position is that of a jailer, while Pio Baroja, through the mouth of a character in his novel "La lucha por la vida," equated the office of executioner with those of priest, military and magistrate, as supports of society. From these supports of society that originated in ancient Roman periods or the societies of that period came the laws we have today in our modern society. The office of executioner as it was back then is still corrupt today. Prison sentences and convictions have been flawed by the way the laws have been written and approved by legislation since here God does not forget to judge and does not turn away his anger here regarding this work of corruption of written decrees by legislative bodies in our world according to Isaiah 10: 1, 2, 3, 4.

In this sense, patricide was considered a particularly infamous crime in ancient Rome (and earlier in Greece), as evidence by the myth of Odeipus (which refers to a conspiracy to kill a parent of the opposite sex and marry either a mother if you are the son or marry either the father if you are the daughter). Here was also is the harshness with which Solon treated it; or the harsh and cruel judgment of the laws formed by the legislative bodies. Here the character of "Tulia the Less" was a figure of unfortunate memory or the memory of an immoral human being that was unlike Tulia. Who here "Tulia" was considered a character having an image of noble stature. And this dignity of "Tulia" who passed on this noble and dignified stature to others and who these others in society may have been impoverished morally by being unjustly labelled as having a notorious or damaged reputation being a low person of stature in society. Here as in almost everything in the monarchical stage, history and legend intertwine. And there remains a mixed narrative of how the youngest daughter of the sixth king, Servius Tullius, not only participated in the conspiracy to assassinate her father and get her second husband, the future Tarquinius the Superb, to ascend the throne, but also desecrated his corpse by driving over it with a chariot. Here a woman who has a character like Servius Tullius and a character like "Tulia" who was the offshoot of the noble Roman Tullius family that represents immoral female children of the Servius Tullius Character as is mentioned and described in the Authorized King James Version Bible according to Proverbs 9: 13, 14, 15, 16, 17, 18. Also the character of " Tulia " is from the moral female children as is mentioned in the Authorized King James Version Bible as well according to Proverbs 31: 10, 11, 12, 13, 14, 15, 16, 17, 18, 19, 20, 21, 22, 23, 24, 25, 26, 27, 28, 29, 30, 31.

It must be understood that the Roman Family was the basic cell of society; it was a vast institution that grouped the members of the family but also those adopted and even servants, and was under the absolute authority of the "pater familias," whose "patria potestas" allowed him to dispose of the lives of all those dependent on him. Therefore, to kill him was revealed as an atrocious act in the personal but also in the social sphere and the state had to act accordingly. The "Lex duodecim tabularum" or "Law of the XII of Tables" defined parricide as the voluntary homicide of parents by their children.

Here in ancient times of the Roman period this legislative corpus or collection of body of evidence was made in the middle of the 5th century B.C. and, with time, the section referring to this type of crime was expanded. This crime of parricide became a trend that was happening more frequently. For example, Lucius Cornelius Sulla, consul between 88 and 80 BC. (with a period of dictatorship from 81 to 80 BC.), extended the possible liability to other relatives in addition to offspring. And the "Lex Pompeia de parricidiis," established by Pompey in 55 B.C., did the same with potential victims, going from being only parents to stepparents, grandparents, siblings, uncles, spouses, cousins, in-laws, sons-in-law, daughters-in-law, stepchildren and even employers. Those who fell outside these categories were governed by the general "Lex Cornelia de sicariis et veneficiis," (which is a law against Murderers and Poisoners) which remained almost unchanged since the XII Tables and punished murder with banishment. Likewise according to "Herennius Modestinus (a Roman jurist of the 3rd century A.D.), the "Lex Pompeia" could be used to accuse parricide in reverse, that is, parents who murdered their children, grandparents who did so with their grandchildren or even anyone who bought poison with the intention of killing their parent, even if they did not actually do it.

Once the crime has been clarified, how does the corresponding punishment arise? It is possible that the origins of the "poena cullei" date back to the monarchic period. During the reign of Tarquinius the Superb, one of the "duumviri sacrorum" or priests which were created by Lucius Tarquinius Superbus; were officers for the performance of sacrifice and keeping of the Sibylline books. They were chosen out of nobility or patricii which means a member of the original hereditary aristocracy of ancient Rome having such privileges as having their exclusive rights to hold certain offices. These were chosen because they were of noble heritage and that this type of "duumviri sacrorum" or priesthood was a false religious or pagan worship of a pagan deity since the true God of the Authorized King James Version Bible has chosen his servants in most cases as those who are not noble and do not come from a noble heritage of descendants but are peasants and are foolish in the eyes of the world but wise in the sight of the true God of the Authorized Kings James Version Bible according to 1st Corinthians 1: 26, 27, 28.

Marcus Atilius who was a "duumviri sacrorum" or priest was appointed to guard the Sibylline Books revealed some of their secrets. So, this was sacrilege because these books were an anthology of prophecies dictated by the "Sibyl of Cumae" and were consulted every time Rome faced a difficult situation to seek possible solutions or guidance; so they were forbidden to the public. So consequently, Marcus Atilius was condemned for revealing these secrets of these Sibylline books and was thrown into the sea inside a sewn sack which was also known as the "poena cullei" or the penalty of the sack. This was sacrilege of this pagan religion because these books were an anthology of prophecies dictated by the "Sibyl of Cumae" which refers to a priestess who presides over the apollonian oracle at cumae a Greek Colony located near Naples Italy and there were many here known as a "Sibyl" which refers to prophetess which there were many of them in different locations throughout the ancient world.

Now, what does that have to do with patricide? Nothing really, unless we believe Dionysius of Halicarnassus, according to whom Atilius was also condemned for parricide. Other authors are of the opinion that he simply took advantage later of that form of execution because of his extravagant character went well to exemplify. Plutarch an ancient philosopher and historian places the date after the Second Punic War which was before the birth of Christ and gives the name of Lucius Hostius as the first documented parricide of Rome, although he does not explain how he was executed; before, the death of a father at the hands of his son would be considered a homicide more, generically.

When it began to give differential category to that type of crime, it would have resorted to the atavistic method of delivering the culprit to the family of the deceased; but being the same, it became necessary to also devise a different punishment. This must have begun towards the end of the third century B.C.; according to some historians, perhaps because of the social disorders that arose among the Romans as a result of the invasion of the Italian peninsula by the Carthaginian Hannibal. They even believe to see in certain passages of Plautus, at the beginning of the following century, humorous references to the introduction of the "poena cullei." These social disorders was a sign that the Romans as a result of the invasion of the Italian peninsula by the Carthaginian Hannibal were on the threshold of the fall of the Roman Empire and therefore those in power took for granted their access to absolute power and authority where here Plautus an ancient comedy writer made fun of the punishments of "poena cullei." The Authorities of the Roman Empire had assumed that they would have a never-ending rule and success in having a large portion of the world under their control and defeating great leaders like general Carthaginian Hannibal. Who Carthaginian Hannibal made to his father that he would never be a friend of Rome. Here the Roman Empire fell on September 4th, 476 A.D. because of the corruption that infected the Roman Empire by those who were in power that took advantage of their widespread power through that western world at that time. It is possible that when the Romans struggled to defeat Carthaginian Hannibal in order to keep their Roman Empire intact that the Roman Empire may have been weakened by their future enemies who learned the lessons of defeat by Carthaginian Hannibal's eventual defeat by the Romans and this may have been part of the reasons for the fall of the Roman Empire on September 4th, 476 AD. So here the Roman Empire was plagued by atrocities who Marcus Atilius was not only the one to go down dying in such an ignominious way. But Plutarch also described the case of a certain Gaius Vilius, who was condemned for having supported the reforms of the Gracchi and who was executed by being locked inside a vase with snakes inside. The Gracchi reform was two Roman brothers named Tiberius Gracchus and Gaius Gracchus who were politicians who tried to reform Rome's social and political structure to help the poor and lower classes in the 2nd century. Both brothers proposed an agricultural reform limiting land ownership to 125 hectares per citizen or 250 hectares per family and distributing the freed-up land to the poorest Romans usually free of charge. These two brothers were politicians who represented the plebs or the common people of the Roman government. The Brothers had followers but a violent uprising took place leading to the deaths of the brothers. Tiberius seeked election where he received enough votes that it led to this violent uprising. Which resulted to Tiberius and Gaius and their followers to be beaten to death.

Other atrocities also included a variant that preceded by a few decades the one that Titus Livius is considered to be the first one to be executed for parricide in the way that would last from then on: Publicius Maleolus, who, having been found guilty of murdering his mother around 100 B.C., was condemned and to be put inside a closed sack and thrown " into a stream of water."

The case of Maleolus is described by various sources and none of them mentions that animals were also introduced with the prisoner, which confirms the current belief that this was a later addition of the first imperial stage of the "poena cullei" penalty. The description that can be read in the "Rhetorica ad Herennium" (Rhetoric to Herennius, an anonymous philosophical treatise dated approximately 90 B.C.), does provide other details, such as that Maleolus' head was covered with wolf-skin bag and soleae lignae (wooden clogs or shoes) were put on him, objects that were intended to isolate the culprit from the world.

However, Cicero (to whom the Rhetoric to Herennius was erroneously attributed for a long time) objects in his "De inventione" that the head bag was made of simple leather, perhaps wineskin. Cicreo speaks several times of "poena cullei" in his writings. For example, in the vibrant speech with which he defended Sextus Roscius against the accusation of murdering his father, but in reality, it was a personal vendetta in which Roscius himself almost died because of the vendetta his father had against him. Here Cicero criticized the system of execution, and incidentally obtained the acquittal of his client.

Suetonius who was a Roman biographer and antiquarian and friend of Pliny or Gaius plinius Caecilius Secundus; the younger; In his work : "The life of Claudius 25" Suetonius mentions how the Emperor Claudius (10 BC - 54 AD) expelled Jews from Rome because of their constant disturbances which he claimed were instigated by Jesus Christ. He also claims that it was Augustus who formally authorized the "poena cullei", although in practice it was already applied, as we saw, and since then it became habitual; so much so that, according to Seneca, in the time of Claudius they saw" more sacks than crosses, from which it would be necessary to deduce that the parricides proliferated. The cross was a deterrent and considered an evil symbol by the secular people of the secular world after Christ was crucified. Here was the reason perhaps why the cross and it's penal punishment had disappeared from the pages of history and that Christianity was abhorred by the secular world where the cross became a religiously divine symbol of God and God's judgments that the secular world would like to deny or forget the events of the miracles of Christ and his resurrection. Here it put a fear in those who preferred to fear man in a reverential way instead of fearing God in a more and serious reverential way according Proverbs 14: 32 and Proverbs 29: 25 and Jeremiah 17: 5.

This subject of parricide had become more frequent than desirable, that it has had its icing on the cake in the death of Agrippina at the hands of her son Nero. Here also Suetonius attributes to the emperor the death of her young lover, Alus Plautius, suspecting that she wanted to replace him on the throne; Later he adds, he did the same to her under the influence of his wife, Poppaea Sabina, fulfilling an ancient prophecy that foretold that he would be emperor, but would kill his mother, to which she would have replied "Occidat, dum imperet" which translated means "Let him kill me as long as he reigns!"

Regardless of whether these facts are true or not, as also happens with the life of the reviled Caligula (Suetonius, one of the main sources for both, belonged to the senatorial class and in that period the Senate struggled not lose its power before the growing imperial authority), and returning to what concern us, Juvenal (Roman Poet) wrote that Nero deserved more punishment than to end up in a sack. Something Suetonius endorses again when he narrates how, after the emperor's suicide, a statue of him appeared partially covered with a "culleum" and accompanied by a writing that read "I did what I could. But you deserve the sack." which here it also refers to "sed tu culleum meruisti" which translated means "but you earned a spoon" which metaphorically means to be lazy and inconsistent to accomplish things and because of this Nero had once also aroused the hatred of everyone around him which therefore led to his suicide.

The "poena cullei" was not only a form of execution. It constituted a whole ritual full of symbols, although not all were incorporated at the same time. Some had antecedents as old as Pharaonic Egypt, where the parricide was martyred by cutting off pieces of flesh with sharpened reeds ad hoc or improvised and burning the martyr on thorns. In this sense, the aforementioned, Modestino, a law scholar in ancient Rome narrates how the prisoner was whipped with the virgae sanguinae (blood sticks, so called because of their function or perhaps because they were previously dyed red), before his head was covered, the clogs were put on him and he was introduced into the sack, whose opening was then sewn; in this way, he was deprived of seeing the sky before dying.

The extra element of the animals inside the sack did not arrive until imperial times. It was precisely Seneca's father who testified to the novelty of the introduction of snakes with the prisoner (specifically a viper, a species believed to kill its parents at birth), while the poet Juvenal, a little later, did the same with respect to a monkey, which embodied madness and was considered a caricatured or a completed distorted and maimed image or version of the human being. It is not clear what other fauna or animal life appeared, perhaps a rooster that is the metaphor of ferocity and violence against its own parents and a dog which is representative of rabies, a despicable animal for the Romans.

In the second century A.D., under Hadrian who was a just emperor of Rome and is recognized as the third of the Five Good Emperors (Nerva, Trajan, Hadrian, Antonius Pius and Marcus Aurelius) who ruled justly. Here we find another faunal element, although not inside the sack: a pair of black oxen pulled the cart that transported the prisoner and his peculiar prison to the water. This had a double meaning; on the one hand, the culprit of such a horrendous crime was deprived of land where he could rest in peace and, on the other hand, the human and animal remains would end up mixed for his eternal dishonor, all of this sifted by the purifying quality attributed to water in the Roman world.

However, with Hadrian the "poena cullei" fell into disuse and became optional; there were other alternatives such as being buried alive or in a "damnatio ad bestias" or translated " Being devoured by wild beasts " in the arena of the amphitheater, although it seems that it applied mainly to lower-class people and it is also unclear whether the condemned could defend themselves from being devoured by wild beasts or awaited their terrible end tied up to face the beast or "obicere bestiis." It is possible that this was to make things easier if there was no body of water nearby, where the beasts would be hungry and thirsty. Two thousand years ago, you could be either thrown to animals, "obicere bestiis" or indulge in "Damnatio ad Bestias," or being devoured by wild beasts where you could actually try to defend yourself against a plethora of animals where a bodily condition characterized by an excess of blood and is marked by turgescent or to be swollen by being a victim of wild beasts such as brown bears, leopards, Caspian tigers or Barbary Lions. It was Roman capital punishment or a religious sacrifice invented around the 2nd century BC. It consisted of Christians or the condemned such as runaway slaves or criminals whose lives were meant to entertain those of the lower class.

However, in the third Century Constantine revitalized the ceremonial -- he was the one who brought the dog and the rooster --- without considering it being incompatible with the new Christian faith. In fact, it was even extended, for in the following century that Constantius included the penalty for adultery and added a fish, as a symbol of lust, to the sack. Here the same happened with Justinian three centuries later, since in his "Institutiones" (an introduction to the legislative compilation he made under the title "Corpus iuris civilis") the "poena cullei" is reflected with all its paraphernalia, including animals. Nevertheless, the "Basilika" (the legal corpus of the Byzantine emperor Leo VI the Wise) shows that in the ninth century it no longer existed and had been replaced by the stake. Here this did not prevent the ceremonial dog and rooster related to the "poena cullei" from being briefly resurrected or brought back into the Middle Ages. For example, it appears in the "Siete Partidas" (a legislative body introduced in the 13th century Castile by King Alfonso X) and with all the characteristics like Sack, Animals, and Water, that although over time it tended to be carried out only metaphorically. The condemned was dragged to the scaffold in a "seron" which is a bale or parcel wrapped in animal hide, usually containing exotic substances and dragged by some beast of burden something here that was continued to be done until the middle of the 19th century and then his corpse was introduced into a bucket that had a dog, a monkey, a rooster and a snake painted on it, and which was simulated to be thrown into the water before burial. But where it really survived was in medieval and modern Germany, as evidence in the 12th century by the

"Sassen Speyghel" (Saxon Mirror) complied in 1235 by Eike von Repgow, may be said to mark the beginning of Vernacular German Juriprudence or the system or body of law. For the first time Maria Dobozy offers an English translation of this influential lawbook, the oldest, and most important, set of customary law in the German language. The most important penal code of the Germanic Middle Ages. There were some differences, however: the rooster was not included, and the serpent was represented only pictorially in a piece of paper and the monkey was replaced with a cat, often separated from the prisoner by a sewn cloth. Moreover, the sack was not made of leather but of linen, which facilitated death by drowning rather than by asphyxiation. This meant shortening the suffering, something that was sometimes sought and sometimes not. A case is recorded in Dresden in which a leather sack waterproofed with pitch was used to make the agony of its occupant last longer. But the sack burst open when it hit water, and the animals were able to escape. The condemned, however, presumably tied, drowned and got his punishment. The last time this punishment was meted out in 1734, somewhere in Saxony. However according to some sources, it could have been that Saxonian city Zittau, where the last case is alleged to have happened in 1749. And in 1761 the "poena cullei" was definitely abolished.

Here is more proof that history tends to constantly either distort or support the truth, therefore it is also interesting to note as I have explained in my last two books in "Pyromancy" and "Magistrates of Damnation" that Constantius included the penalty for adultery that was a fish that was put in a sack with the condemned culprit. That here also the fish can be fatal if it is eaten by those who drank blood and water by faith in order to receive the Holy Spirit. Although fish was a symbol of reverence for God and to be eaten by those of the Catholic Christian faith towards God and to be eaten by those who practiced the Catholic Christian faith on the day of the Crucifixion of Christ; which was considered to be on a Friday according to the Catholic Church which in reality Christ was Crucified on Wednesday as I go into detail about this in my book " Pyromancy " and " Magistrates of Damnation. " It is after all this ---- that it has been, and still is to be considered a complete abomination to God to continue to practice this type of abominable and futile sacrifice of eating fish and abstaining from meat. Which refers to worshipping idols like the virgin Mary and eating fish instead of fasting as Christ says is to be done in Matthew 6: 25. And how eating this fish on a pagan day of Friday is sacrificing onto an idol like the virgin Mary the mother of Jesus or Jesus himself in an unlawful law of apostasy and disrespect towards Christ and his sacrifice and what he stands for.

The "Lex Pompeia" was an application used on Parricides to those who defrauded the nation. Just as the Romans, he argued, face to face with a monstrous and unprecedented crime, devised for it a monstrous and unprecedented punishment, so the British were invited to tie the directors of the South Sea Company into sacks with a dog , a cock, a viper, and an ape in each and sink them in the Thames river. The statement then made is, it seems, the general belief about the origin of this famous Roman death penalty is that this belief is demonstrably wrong, although Seneca, who doubles knew better, makes a rhetorical point by pretending to share it.

Parricide did not first occur in Rome in the first pre-Christian century, nor was tying in a sack and subsequent drowning first introduced then. Both the offence and this particular mode of vindicating it; were ancient. It is also possible that before the crucifixion of Christ that these ancient laws were considered honorable. But after the Romans and the Pharisees had Christ crucified for healing people and being falsely accused of blaspheme against God when the religious institution of the Pharisees were apostate in nature; people assumed that these laws that the Romans and Pharisees abided by were completely vague without any significant deterrent to judge those who were guilty of an legitimate crime and did not vindicate those who were not as guilty of a felony but a lesser crime or who possibly were innocent of a crime.

Here people of that time took advantage of these laws that were vague and took it upon themselves to go out and commit parricide and random murder. Furthermore the justice system of that time took it upon themselves as well to punish those who were found guilty of a crime; or even if there was a lack of evidence ---- or they may have in reality been innocent or guilty of a lesser crime that they may have used tactics of penalties of a monstrousness nature and to punish them by the legal system they had back then. So, after the penalty of "poena cullei" was implemented the deterrent to commit parricide and murder was weak before crucifixion was thought of and implemented. But the crucifixion penalty or punishment was also given a bad name because the Son of God was crucified without a cause as a fully innocent man. This was a perverted way of dealing within the realm of true justice according to Deuteronomy 24: 16, 17. Here this type of perverted justice is unjustified and cursed by those people who place their trust in God by expressing "Amen" and also cursed by God as well since Christ was betrayed as an innocent man by Judas who took the reward of thirty pieces of silver according to Matthew 26: 14, 15, 16 and according to Deuteronomy 27: 19, 25, 26. Here Judas Iscariot was perhaps cursed by God for the betrayal of Jesus Christ and tried to go back to repentance after being tormented by demons by returning back to his house of morality he once possessed and in the end Judas Iscariot was so severely tormented by these demons sent by God as a curse on him that he hung himself according to Luke 11: 24, 25, 26 and Matthew 27: 1, 2, 3, 4, 5.

Also, the prison murder and death of Richard Albert Loeb on January 28th / 1936, usually referred to collectively as Leopold and Loeb or known as Nathan Freudenthal Leopold Jr. Born November 19th / 1904 to his death of August 29th / 1971 and Richard Albert Loeb Born June 11th / 1905 to his murder and death of January 28th / 1936. Leopold and Loeb were two wealthy students at the University of Chicago who kidnapped and murdered 14-year-old Bobby Franks in Chicago, Illinois United States, in May 1924. They committed the murder --- characterized at the time as the crime of the century --- hoping to demonstrate superior intellect, which they believed enabled and entitled them to carry out a perfect crime without consequences.

After the two were arrested, Loeb's family retained Clarence Darrow as lead counsel for their defense. Darrow's twelve-hour summation at their sentencing hearing is noted for its influential criticism of capital punishment as retributive rather than transformative justice. Both young men were sentence to life imprisonment plus 99 years. Loeb was murdered by a fellow prisoner in 1936. Leopold was released on parole in 1958. The case has since served as the inspiration for several dramatic works.

Nathan Leopold was born on Noveber 19th / 1904, in Chicago, Illinois, the son of Florence (nee' Foreman) and Nathan Leopold, a wealthy German-Jewish immigrant family. A child prodigy or an extraordinarily talented child at an early age Nathan Freudenthal Leopold Jr. was claimed to have spoken his first words at the age of four months. At the time of the murder, he had completed an undergraduate degree at the University of Chicago with Phi Beta Kappa honors --- the " Phi Beta Kappa Society " is the oldest academic honor society in the United States and the most prestigious, due in part to its long history and academic selectivity. Phi Beta Kappa aims to promote and advocate excellence in the liberal arts and sciences. Also, Nathan Leopold Jr. had planned to begin studies at Harvard Law School after a trip to Europe.

Unlike the handsome, athletic Richard Albert Loeb, Leopold was undersized, with rather bulging eyes. By many accounts, he was sensitive about his appearance. Leopold threw himself into intellectual pursuits where he was met with remarkable success. Leopold had reportedly studied fifteen languages and claimed to speak five fluently. He had achieved a measure of national recognition as an ornithologist, (the study and research of birds). Leopold and several other ornithologists identified the Kirtland's warbler and made astute observations about the parasitic nesting behavior of "brown headed cowbirds," which threatened the warblers. He maintained his interest in birds after his crime, writing to the Field Museum from his prison cell regarding specimens he had donated.
 Richard Albert Loeb was born on June 11th / 1905, in Chicago, the second of four sons of Anna Henrietta (nee' Bohnen) and Albert Henry Loeb, a wealthy lawyer and retired vice president of Sears, Roebuck & Company. His father was Jewish and his mother was Catholic. Like Leopold, Loeb was exceptionally intelligent. He was an avid reader, with a passion for historical novels and crime stories. At age 12, he entered the innovative University High School. With the encouragement of his governess, he completed his high school education in two years. He would later go on to become the University of Michigan's youngest graduate at age 17. Following graduation from Michigan, Loeb enrolled in a course in constitutional history at the University of Chicago Law School. At the time of the murder, he was especially interested in doing graduate work in history. Loeb was not strictly intellectual as Leopold. he often socialized, played tennis, and read detective novels.

The two young men Leopold and Loeb grew up with their families in the affluent Kenwood neighbourhood on Chicago's South Side. The Loeb's owned a summer estate (now called Castle Farms) in Charlevoix, Michigan, as well as a mansion in Kenwood, two blocks from the Leopold home.

Though Leopold and Loeb knew each other casually while growing up, they began to see more of each other in the mid 1920's, and their relationship flourished at the University of Chicago, particularly after they discovered a mutual interest in crime. Leopold was particularly fascinated by Fried Nietzsche --- a philosopher whose work has exerted a profound influence on contemporary philosophy and Fried Nietzsche's concept of superman which was also referred to as "Ubermenschen" a concept that represents a shift from other secular Christian values to the Ubermenschen's secularism that manifests the grounded human ideal regarding the means of super-human or beyond human strength or out of proportion to humanity. Here Leopold interpreted this so-called superman ----- as transcendent individuals possessing extraordinary and unusual capabilities, whose superior intellects allowed them to rise above the laws and rules that bound unimportant, average populace.

Leopold believed that he and Loeb were such individuals, and as such, by his interpretation of Nietzsche's doctrines, that they were not bound by any of society's normal ethics or rules. In a letter to Loeb, he wrote, "A superman... is on account of certain superior qualities inherent in him, exempted from the ordinary laws which govern men. He is not liable for anything he may do." Here Leopold is a prime example of someone who is boastful and proud and not having humility towards others and also of not having the means to grasp what is right from wrong or not accepting reproof or getting criticism for a fault according Proverbs 15: 31, 32, 33.
The pair began to asserting their perceived immunity from normal restrictions with acts of petty theft and vandalism. Breaking into a fraternity house at the University of Michigan, they stole penknives, a camera, and a typewriter that they later used to type the ransom note for their murder victim, Bobby Franks. Emboldened, they progressed to a series of more serious crimes, including arson, but no one seemed to notice. Disappointed with the absence of media coverage of their crimes, they decided to plan and execute a sensational " perfect crime " that would garner public attention and confirm their self-perceived status as "supermen."

Leopold and Loeb who were 19 and 18, respectively, at the time, settled on kidnapping and murdering a younger adolescent as their "perfect Crime." They spent seven months planning everything, from the method of abduction to disposal of the body. To obfuscate or darken and make the actual nature of their crime and motive obscure, they decided to make a ransom demand, and devised an intricate plan for collecting this ransom involving a long series of complex instructions to be communicated, one set at a time, by phone. They typed the final set of instructions involving the actual money drop in the form of a ransom note, using the typewriter stolen from the fraternity house. A chisel was selected as the murder weapon and purchased.

After a Lengthy search for a suitable victim, mostly on the grounds of the Harvard School for Boys in the Kenwood area, where Leopold had been educated, the pair decided upon Robert "Bobby" Franks, the 14-year-old son of wealthy Chicago watch manufacturer Jacobs Franks. Bobby Franks was Loeb's second cousin and an across-the-street neighbour who had played tennis at the Loeb residence several times.

Leopold and Loeb put their plan in motion on the afternoon of May 21, 1924. Using an automobile, the Leopold rented under the name Morton D. Ballard, they offered Franks a ride as he walked home from school. The boy initially refused, because his destination was less than two blocks away, but Loeb persuaded him to enter the car to discuss a tennis racket that he had been using. The precise sequence of the events that followed remains in dispute, but a preponderance of opinion placed Leopold behind the wheel of the car while Loeb sat in the back seat with the chisel. Loeb struck Franks, who was sitting in front of him in the passenger seat, several times in the head with the chisel, then dragged him into the back seat and gagged him, where he eventually died. With the body on the floorboard of the car and out of view, the men drove to their predetermined dumping spot near Wolf Lake in Hammond, Indiana, 25 miles (40 km) south of Chicago. Wolf lake is an 804-acre (325.4 ha) lake that straddles the Indiana and Illinois state line near Lake Michigan. It is smaller than it was prior to settlement by European colonizers because of infilling for development around the edges. Despite years of environmental damage caused by heavy industries. Because of this damage Wolf Lake may have been a desolate place where the public may have rarely attended the lake. Making it a perfect dumping ground for a dead body.

After nightfall, they removed and discarded Franks' clothes, then concealed the body in a culvert. A culvert is a structure that channels water past an obstacle or a subterranean waterway. A culvert may be made by a large concrete pipe or reinforced concrete or other material. The size of a culvert could be big enough to place a body in or you can crawl or walk into a culvert. This culvert was along the Pennsylvania Railroad tracks north of the lake. To obscure the body's identity, they poured hydrochloric acid on the face and genitals to disguise the fact that he had been circumcised.

By the time the two men returned to Chicago, word had already spread that Franks was missing. Leopold called Franks' mother, identifying himself as "George Johnson," and told her that Franks had been kidnapped; instructions for delivering the ransom would follow. After mailing the typed ransom note and burning their blood-stained clothing, then cleaning the blood stains from the rented vehicle's upholstery, they spent the remainder of the evening playing cards.

Once the Franks family received the ransom note on the following morning, Leopold called a second time and dictated the first set of instructions for the ransom payment. The intricate plan stalled almost immediately when a nervous family member forgot the address of the store where he was supposed to receive the next set of directions, and it was abandoned entirely when word came that Frank's body had been found. Leopold and Loeb destroyed the typewriter and burned a car robe (lap blanket) they had used to move the body. Then they went about their lives as usual.

Chicago police launched an intensive investigation; rewards were offered for information. While Loeb went about his daily routine quietly, Leopold spoke freely to police and reporters, offering theories to anyone who would listen. He even told one detective, "If I were to murder anybody, it would be just such a cocky little son of a bitch as Bobby Franks."
Police found a pair of eyeglasses near Franks body. Although common in prescription and frame, they were fitted with an unusual hinge purchased by only three customers in Chicago, one of them was Leopold. When questioned, Leopold offered the possibly that his glasses might have dropped out of his pocket during bird- watching trip the previous weekend. Leopold and Loeb were summoned for formal questioning on May 29 /

1924. They asserted that on the night of the murder, they had picked up two women in Chicago using Leopold's car, then dropped them off some time later near a golf course without learning their last names. Their alibi was exposed as a fabrication when Leopold's chauffeur told police that he was repairing Leopold's car while the men claimed to be using it. The chauffeur's wife confirmed that the car was parked in the Leopold garage on the night of the murder. The destroyed typewriter was recovered from the Jackson Park Lagoon on June 7 / 1924.

Loeb was the first to confess. He asserted that Leopold had planned everything and had killed Franks in the back seat of the car while he (Loeb) drove. Leopold's confession followed swiftly thereafter. He insisted that he was the driver and Loeb was the murderer. Their confessions otherwise corroborated most of the evidence in the case. Both confessions were announced by the state's attorney on May 31 / 1924.

Leopold later claimed, long after Loeb was dead, that he pleaded in vain with Loeb to admit to killing Franks. Mompsie (or Bobby Franks' mother) feels less terrible than she might, thinking you did it, he quotes Loeb as saying, "and I'm not going to take that shred of comfort away from her." Most observers believed that Loeb did strike the fatal blows. Some circumstantial evidence -- including testimony from eyewitness Carl Ulvigh, who said that he saw Loeb driving and Leopold in the back-seat minutes before the kidnapping --- suggested that Leopold could have been the killer.

 Here Leopold was undersized, with rather bulging eyes. While Loeb was handsome and athletic. By many accounts Leopold was sensitive about his appearance regarding being undersized and with having rather bulging eyes. Is it possible that for this reason he may have been an outcast with women and with some or most men that he had a motive to plan everything about this murder since his comment calling Bobby Franks quote "such a cocky little son of a bitch" may have most people suspect that he was enraged enough to kill him where Booby Franks may have been a 14 year old ladies' man? Where this jealousy and envy on Leopold's part was evident according to Galatians 5: 21 and 2nd Corinthians 12: 20 and James 3: 14, 15, 16 and Proverbs 6: 34, 35.

Both Leopold and Loeb admitted that were driven by their thrill-seeking and their obsessions with Supermen delusions of "Ubermenschen" and their aspiration or a strong desire to achieve something high or great in profile regarding media attention. Committing the perfect crime where they would get media attention for the crime and be exposed as the perpetrators of this crime in the media; but either would not be charged for the crime or be acquitted in a courtroom making for even greater media attention. But here neither Leopold nor Loeb were to have claimed to look forward to the killing. But Leopold admitted interest in learning what it would feel like to be a murderer. He was disappointed to note that he felt the same as ever.

Here this ransom attempt of this crime which took place on Wednesday May 21st / 1924, took place with 14-year-old Bobby Franks who was walking by himself home from school. A car stopped and a familiar face appeared in its open window. Bobby got into the car and the car raced away. Around dinner time, Bobby had not come home nor had he contacted his parents, Jacob and Flora Franks. His brother Jack and his sister Josephine had no idea where he was. Perhaps he was playing tennis at the Loeb's, Jack suggested. But when his father looked over at the Loeb's tennis court, Bobby was nowhere to be seen.

While Flora called Bobby's classmates, Jacob contacted the headmaster of the school to find out if Bobby could have gotten himself locked in school building. He called Samuel Ettelson, a prominent lawyer and friend, to determine what to do. Ettelson and Jacob searched the entire school building, but found no sign of Bobby. While they were gone, Flora got a phone call. A man calling himself Johnson told her, "Your son has been kidnapped. He is all right. There will be further news in the morning." Flora fainted and remained unconscious until her husband and Ettelson came home. At two in the morning, Jacob and Ettelson went to the police, but since none of the police officials that Ettelson knew were on duty at that hour, they decided to come back later that morning.

The Franks were residents of Kenwood, a wealthy neighbourhood in Chicago. They lived quietly among Jewish elite of Kenwood, but had not been accepted socially for several reasons. They had renounced their Jewish faith to become Christian Scientists. Jacob had made much of his money running a pawnshop which didn't recommend them socially to the powerful Jewish executives, bankers and attorneys in the neighbourhood. Here is also a sign that possibly these Jewish elite who were wealthy executives, bankers and attorneys who were the modern Pharisees of this period in history since the Pharisees 2,000 years ago had Christ crucified. So these Jewish elites of the neighbourhood may have had some sort of grudge against the Franks for their Christian faith in God according to John 8 : 37, 38, 39, 40, 41, 42, 43, 44, 45, 46, 47, 48, 49.

The next morning, the mailman arrived with a special delivery letter:

Dear Sir: As you no doubt know by this time your son has been kidnapped. Allow us to assure he is present well and safe. You need fear no physical harm for him, provided you live up carefully to the following instructions and to such others as you will receive by future communications. Should you, however, disobey any of our instructions, even slightly, his death will be the penalty.

1. For obvious reasons make absolutely no attempt to communicate with either police authorities or any private agency. Should you already have communicated with the police, allow them to continue their investigations, but do not mention this letter.
2. Secure before noon today $10,000. This money must be composed entirely of old bills of the following denominations: $2,000 in $20 bills, $8,000 in $50 bills. The money must be old. Any attempt to include new or marked bills will render the entire venture futile.
3. The money should be placed in a large cigar box, or if this is impossible, in a heavy cardboard box, securely closed and wrapped in white paper. The wrapping paper should be sealed at all openings with sealing wax.
4. Have the money with you, prepared as directed above, and remain at home after one o'clock. See that the telephone is not in use.

It was signed "George Johnson" and guaranteed that if the money were delivered according to his instructions that Bobby would be returned unharmed.

While Jacob went to get the money, Ettelson called his friend who was chief of detectives for the Chicago Police Department. An enterprising newspaperman had been tipped off that there was a kidnapping involving the Franks' boy. He had also heard that a boy had been found dead in a culvert near Wolf Lake, a probable drowning victim. He relayed the description of the dead boy to Mr. Franks, who did not think it matched his son. Frank's brother-in-law went to check it out.

When the phone rang, "George Johnson" told Ettelson, "I am sending a Yellow Cab for you. Get in and go to the drugstore at 1465 East Sixty-third Street." Ettelson handed the phone to Jacob and the message was repeated. In the trauma of the events, both men immediately forgot the address of the drugstore.

The phone rang again. This time it was Jacob's brother-in-law. The boy that had been found dead----- in the culvert was Bobby Franks.

The investigation of Bobby Franks' death went into high gear. Unfortunately, an opportunity was lost when Jacobs Franks and Samuel Ettelson forgot the address of the drugstore where they were to await instructions from the kidnapper. Soon a Yellow Cab arrived at the Franks' home, sent by the kidnapper, but the driver had not been given any instructions as to the destination.

Shortly afterwards, at the Van de Bogert & Ross drugstore on East Sixty-third Street, a phone call came in for a Mr. Franks. The caller was told that there was no Mr. Franks there. A few minutes later, another call came for Mr. Franks, along with a description of Jacob Franks. The druggist told the caller that there was no man in the store of that description. The culvert near Wolf Lake in which the body of Bobby Franks was found near railroad tracks. Here also were the members of the railroad crew who found the body and that had lifted the naked body of Bobby Franks. Bobby's clothes were not found nearby, but a pair of eyeglasses were lying on the ground.

The ransom note was written here by someone well educated:

Dear Sir: Proceed immediately to the back platform of the train. Watch the east side of the track. Have your package ready. Look for the first LARGE, RED, BRICK, factory situated immediately adjoining the tracks on the east. On top of this factory is a large, black water tower with the word CHAMPION written on it. Wait till you have COMPLETELY passed the south

The police focused upon three teachers at the Harvard School where Bobby Franks attended, they were taken to the police station and grilled for hours while their apartments were searched. One of the teachers was released. but the other two were kept in custody.

The small horn-rimmed glasses found near the body did not belong to the boy. The frames, which were made of Xylonite, and were chewed at the ends. The prescription was very common. The chances of finding the owner of the glasses seemed slim, but every attempt was made. The newspapers carried photos of the glasses and the police contacted optical companies in the area.

On Friday, May 23, Richard Loeb a handsome nineteen-year-old University of Chicago student and neighbour of the Franks family was at his Zeta Beta Tau fraternity house with Howard Mayer who was the campus Liaison to the "Evening American." Loeb suggested that they try to locate the drugstore that the kidnapper had instructed Jacob Franks to go to with the ransom money. Just as the two of them were about to check the various drugstores, two "Daily News" reporters, one of whom was Zeta Beta Tau member, came into the fraternity house and decided to go with them.

Eventually, they found the Van de Bogert & Ross drugstore and confirmed that there had been two calls the previous day for Mr. Franks. "This is the place!" Loeb Shrieked enthusiastically to the others. "This is what comes from reading detective stories." Mulroy, one of the reporters, asked Loeb if he knew the murdered boy. Loeb told him he had, then he smiled and said, "If I were going to murder anybody, I would murder just such a cocky little son of a bitch as Bobby Franks."

On Friday the 23rd, the coroner's inquest was held. Dr Joseph Springer had conducted the autopsy. Bobby Franks had died of suffocation, perhaps when his kidnapper held his hand over the boy's mouth or when he had shoved something down the boy's throat. There were a number of wounds on the boy's body which suggested that he had fought with his captor.

There were small wounds on the right and left sides of his head, plus bleeding and bruises from a blunt instrument on Bobby's forehead. Some chemical had been poured on his face and penis. While there was dome dilation of the rectum, Springer said that Bobby had not been sexually abused. When police talked to the game warden for the area around Wolf Lake, they found that one frequent visitor to the area was Nathan Leopold, a nineteen-year-old ornithologist. Police had a servant awaken the young man so that he could come down to the police station for questioning. Young Nathan Leopold was questioned, but the answers he gave about his birdwatching expeditions were very credible and he did not arouse suspicion.

The Leopold's were a very highly respected family of German Jews who had arrived in the United States in the Mid- 1800's. The family had made its fortune transporting grain, minerals and other freight on the Great Lakes. They lived in the same wealthy Kenwood area as the Franks family.
A cabdriver came forward with the story of two well-dressed young men who hired him to drive them to the home of Jacob Franks. Once there, the two men sat in the cab for several minutes, but did not get out. He then drove them to another destination.

Eight days after the murder, police discovered that the hinges on the pair of eyeglasses were very unique and had only been sold on three pairs of glasses in the Chicago area. One of those three pairs of glasses belonged to Nathan Leopold.

After this scenario of these glasses and the fact they were found at the crime scene. Both Leopold and Loeb were arrested and a trial date had been set. The trial of Leopold and Loeb at Chicago's Cook County Criminal Court became a media spectacle and the third --- after those of crimes committed by Harry Thaw and Sacco and Vanzetti --- was to be labeled "the trial of the century." Loeb's family hired the renowned criminal defense attorney Clarence Darrow to lead the defense team. It was rumoured that Darrow was paid 1 million dollars for his services, but he was actually paid 70,000 dollars equivalent to 1,200,000 dollars in 2022. Darrow took the case because he was a staunch opponent of capital punishment.

While it was generally assumed that the men's defense would be based on a plea of not guilty by reason of insanity, Darrow concluded that a jury trial would almost certainly end in conviction and the death penalty. Thus, he elected to enter a plea of guilty, hoping to convince Cook County Circuit Court John R. Caverly to impose sentences of life imprisonment.

In January 28th / 1936, Loeb was attacked by fellow inmate James Day with a straight razor in a shower room; he died soon after in the prison hospital. Day claimed that Loeb had sexually assaulted him, but he was unharmed while Loeb sustained more than fifty wounds, including defensive wounds on his arms and hands. His throat had been slashed from behind. News accounts suggested Loeb had propositioned Day; the authorities, perhaps embarrassed by alleged same-sex behaviour in the prison, ruled that Day was defending himself.

A sexual motive for the killing was suggested. While some sources state that newsman Ed Lahey began his story in the Chicago Daily News with the lead, " Richard Loeb, despite his erudition or his prudent or bookish knowledge, today ended his sentence with a proposition " --- no evidence has been found that this lead was ever published, and an actual copy from that date reads otherwise.

On February 19th / 1936, in a column printed in the Syracuse Journal, Mark Hellinger wrote, "I must tell you of the line that came to me from an unknown correspondent in Chicago. This anonymous contributor said he had the absolute low-down on the recent slaying of Dickie Loeb." Seems that Loeb was a sexual predator while in prison, but Day was later caught at least once in a sexual act with a fellow inmate. In his autobiography, "Life Plus 99 years," Leopold ridiculed Day's claim that Loeb had attempted to sexually assault him. This was echoed by the prison's Catholic chaplain, a confidant of Loeb's who said that it was more likely that Day attacked Loeb after Loeb rebuffed his advances.

Here we read of Darrow's speech in he made to the Judge in court for the leniency of the conviction and punishment of the sentences of Nathan Leopold Jr. and Richard Loeb:
Darrow's impassioned, twelve-hour long "masterful plea" and at the conclusion of the hearing has been called the finest speech of his career. Its principal arguments were that methods and punishments of the American justice system were inhumane, and the youth and immaturity of the accused. This terrible crime was inherent in his organism, and it came from some ancestor. Is any blame attached because somebody took Nietzsche's philosophy seriously and fashioned his life upon it? It is hardly fair to hang a 19-year-old boy for the philosophy that was taught him at the university.

We read of killing one hundred thousand men a day during World War I. We read about it and we rejoice in it-- if it was the other fellows who were killed. We were fed on flesh and drank blood. Even down to the pratting babe. I need not tell you how many upright, honorable young boys have come into this court charged with murder, some saved and some sent to their death, boys who fought in this war and learned to place a cheap value on human life. You know it and I know it. These boys were brought up in it.

It will take fifty years to wipe it out of the human heart, if ever. I know this, that after the Civil War in 1865, crimes of this sort increased, marvelously. No one needs to tell me that crime has no cause. It has as definite a cause as any other disease, and I know that out of the hatred and bitterness of the Civil War crime increased as America had never seen before. I know that Europe is going through the same experience today; I know it has followed every war; and I know it has influenced these boys so that life was not the same to them as it would have been if the world had not made red with blood.

Your Honor knows that in this very court crimes of violence have increased growing out of the war. Not necessarily by those who fought, but by those that learned that blood was cheap, and human life was cheap, and if the State could take it lightly why not the boy?

Has the court any right to consider anything but these two boys? The State says that your Honor has a right to consider the welfare of the community as you have. If the welfare of the community would be benefited by taking these lives, well and good. I think it would work evil and that no one could measure. Has your Honor a right to consider the families of these defendants? I have been sorry, and I am sorry for the bereavement of Mr. and Mrs. Franks, for those broken ties that cannot be healed. All I can hope and wish is that some good may come from it all. But as compared with families of Leopold and Loeb, the Franks are to be envied --- and everyone knows it.

Here is Leopold's father-- and this boy was the pride of his life. He watched him and he cared for him, he worked for him; the boy was brilliant and accomplished. He educated him, and he thought that fame and position awaited him, as it should have awaited. It is a hard thing for a father to see his life's hopes crumble into dust.

And Loeb's the same. Here are the faithful uncle and brother, who have watched here day by day, while Dickie's Father and his mother are too ill to stand this terrific strain, and shall be waiting for a message which means more to them than it can mean to you or me. Shall these be taken into account in this general bereavement?

The easy thing and the popular thing to do is to hang my clients. I know it.

Men and women who do not think will applaud. The cruel and thoughtless will approve. It will be easy today; but in Chicago, and reaching out over the length and breadth of the land, more and more fathers and mothers, the humane, the kind and the hopeful, who are gaining an understanding and asking questions not only about these poor boys, but about their own --- these will join in no acclaim at the death of my clients.

These would ask that the shedding of blood be stopped, and that the normal feelings of man resume their sway. Your Honor stands between the past and the future. You may hang these boys; you may hang them by the neck until they are dead. But in doing it you will turn your face toward the past. In doing it you are making it harder for every other boy who in ignorance and darkness must grope his way through the mazes which only childhood knows. In doing it you make it harder for unborn children. You may save them and make it easier for every child that someone may stand where these boys stand. You will make it easier for every human being with an aspiration and a vision and a hope and a fate. I am pleading for the future; I am pleading for a time when hatred and cruelty will not control the hearts of men. When we can learn by reason and judgment and understanding and faith that all life is worth saving, and mercy is the highest attribute of man.

The judge was persuaded, but he explained in his ruling that his decision was based primarily on precedent and the youth of the accused. On September 10th / 1924, he sentenced both Leopold and Loeb to life imprisonment for the murder, and an additional 99 years for the kidnapping. A little over a month later, Loeb's father died of heart failure.
Were the families of Leopold and Loeb envied? Did Bobby Franks deserve to die? Was he a cocky little son of a bitch? Did Nathan Leopold Jr. and Richard Loeb deserve leniency in the conviction and sentence of this crime? Where does humanity draw the line on being lenient with a perpetrator of a cold-blooded crime like murder? Was Bobby Franks a cold-blooded killing? Was Bobby responsible also for his possible arrogant and boastful behaviour that may have led to his murder according to Proverbs 27: 1, 2. So was the conviction and sentence that has excluded the execution of

Leopold and Loeb resulting in only life in prison justified? These types of sins that involve boasting and envy and jealousy and greed and immediate wrath has destroyed the fabric of our societies and countries worldwide. That would otherwise be a moral presence in our world avoiding bloodshed and wars that have gone on for centuries that has accumulated to millenary history of violence dating back to the time of Genesis. Nothing here can be further from the truth.

Here the term "perfect crime" refers to committing a crime that is not detected by forensic investigative authorities or not having the presence of evidence at the crime scene or the persons involved in; such as a murder victim or having potential witnesses at the crime scene or having knowledge of who the perpetrators may be. Nathan Leopold Jr. and Richard Loeb were so arrogant that they had character traits to the similarities of Donald Trump's character who were seeking media attention and media coverage for their petty crimes. And that when they failed at getting this attention from the media that they moved on and graduated from the fear of committing misdemeanor crimes to the crime of a felony such as murder after overcoming their fear of committing a petty crimes and seeing possibly a few months in jail if they were caught for these petty crimes. They thought that they had the potential to succeed or thought that they would be recognized and being really something in the media by not getting caught for this crime they had committed which was the murder of Bobby Franks and which was considered a cold-blooded felony. Yet they were deceived by their own arrogance and pride and boastful attitude -- and thinking that they were supermen who also believed in Nietzsche's Philosophy and believed in having an invincible intellect and superior intelligence who would not get caught for this murder of Bobby Franks or be not convicted if they were put on trial for it, according to Galatians 6: 3, 4, 5, 6, 7.

CHAPTER 4
RETRIBUTION FOR DEATH

Revenge is an act that has been around since the existence of sin that infiltrated this planet of ours with blood shed. Revenge has been committed in situations like love triangles or love relationships gone bad. Also bad monetary business deals that have gone so bad, that a person who had a significant amount of money all of the sudden lost his earnings that he or she saved up for years, only to lose it by trusting a person or even a close friend whom they placed blind trust in, and they took them for a fool where they either were robbed by them deceitfully, or were involved with them in a business investment that went wrong. Sometimes it was either because this person or close friend whom they got involved with; was either negligent with their money or they wanted to profit off their money they had invested in with them leaving them in the end bankrupt or even dead by assassination. Or even a corporation that became jeopardized because of the way the person who was murdered conducted their business in corrupt manner in the corporate world. These stories are some of these examples mentioned in this paragraph of business deals gone bad, and love relationships that have gone wrong and love triangles that caused severe problems like murder according to the following:

The story of Barry and Honey Sherman murders was a story that captivated the world's attention for recognizing that the morals or the immoral handling of business affairs by the Sherman's. They were criticized for their obsession with business and money so much so that Barry Sherman was so obsessed about it that he was a workaholic. On the other hand, Honey Sherman was that social force that propelled the business of pharmaceutical drugs they were in. Here some drugs may have been not been at a reasonable price for the disabled and low-income recipients of these pharmaceutical drugs. Or some drugs may have been approved by the FDA that may have been harmful like some, if not most psychiatric drugs, or other pharmaceutical drugs that were brought to the market since the term "sorcery" and "sorcerers" according to the "The Strong's Exhaustive Concordance of the Bible" New Testament # 5331 from # 5332 here refers to "medication" "pharmacy" "magic" (literally or figuratively) or "sorcery," or   "witchcraft" or "spell giving potion" a "druggist"   or "poisoner" or a "magician" or "sorcerer" according to Revelation 21: 8 and Revelation 22: 15.

It's been just over 5 years at the time of this writing since Billionaire couple Barry and Honey Sherman were found dead in their Toronto home. Their necks fastened with belts tied to a railing. To this day, the circumstances surrounding their murders remain a mystery.

Barry the founder and CEO of the generic drug manufacturer Apotex, was one of Canada's richest people. Honey was a philanthropist, serving on the boards of numerous charities. The mystery of their deaths has led to rampant public speculation. Some believe it was a business deal gone wrong, or a hit job ordered by a big Pharma rival. Others contend the murders were likely personal --- closer to home.

The Shermans were very complicated people who had reputations, personalities that were very polarizing within themselves, host Kathleen Goldhar told CBC podcasts. The series features people who knew the Shermans well, and even the words of Barry himself, read by actor Saul Rubinek. While the crime remains unsolved the series explores different theories around their deaths and offers listeners a chance to come to their own conclusions.

People are fascinated by this couple and their deaths. I mean, they are billionaires. People are always curious and fascinated by wealthy people. We knew it was coming up on the fifth-year anniversary. The police are nowhere closer to finding out what happened to this couple than they were that day that they died. And I think that people and journalists alike who's interested in public good, having a police investigation that hasn't figured this out, it is also important to shine some light on it.

But also, just as somebody who lives in the city, who's in the Jewish community, who is also fascinated by wealth, are fascinated by how their family has fallen apart and what it means to have that kind of money. And then when you die, there are so many questions and potential suspects. What kind of life do you have and that you have lived that many people could have wanted you dead? We only have the possible theory that the Shermans were too open with their business dealings where some people who disapproved of their corrupt handling of money and pharmaceutical drugs had them and their foolish lips that revealed of their evil works to their adversaries leading them to being murdered in the end according to Proverbs 15: 7.

 Also were their murders an indirect judgment of God of the Shermans being rejecting Jews of the Bible? And the fact that Barry Sherman was an atheist who may have rejected Christ with all the money that he had. And became so indulged in his prosperity that he had earned. Claiming that he has blessed himself and may have been guilty in the sight of God? Like the Jewish chief priests known also as the Pharisees of Christ's time where they had Christ persecuted and crucified because of their atheism against Christ's words and against the words of Christ's God the Father according to: John 19: 6, 7, 8, 9 ,10, 11, 12, 13, 14, 15.

John Wayne Bobbit the notorious revenge victim where his wife who was the predator in this crime of vengeance against him who complained of years of spousal abuse from him was absolutely astonishing. The concept of revenge is as old as history. Almost since the dawn of recorded history, humans had the desire to exact vengeance on others who have committed an offensive act of betrayal against those who placed their loyalty and their trust in the person who betrayed them or have committed and offensive breach or act against them either in a friendship or a business deal involving money or in a love relationship. Here for example the "Code of Hammurabi" the code of law from the sixth king of Babylon, was implemented about 1760 C.E., making it the oldest recorded set of laws in human history. The code is rooted firmly in the belief in an eye for an eye; in fact, that's almost exactly how the concept was phrased.

Back in June 1993, Lorena Bobbitt made the headlines after she cut off her husband's penis with a carving knife as he slept. The former Mrs. Bobbitt alleges that her ex-husband victimized her, using physical violence and even marital rape as a means of maintaining control over her. In 1993, on the night she got her revenge, she says John Wayne Bobbitt came home intoxicated, then assaulted and raped her. After he fell asleep, retrieved a carving knife from their kitchen and used it to remove his penis. She left the house with the severed organ in her hand and drove for 15 minutes, before tossing it out the driver's side window, and then fleeing to the nearby nail salon where she worked, as she recalled in a 2019 New York Times article. She later told police the location where she had discarded the penis. After searching in the roadside grass, the officers found the penis and put it on ice in a hot dog box from a convenience store, and rushed it to the hospital. In a nine-and-a-half-hour operation, the penis was surgically reattached to John Wayne Bobbitt.

Lorena Bobbitt alleged that she had cut off her husband's penis after he had sexually assaulted her. Both ended being charged in relation to the incident. John Wayne Bobbitt was charged with marital sexual assault, charges that his lawyer argued were untrue, and was acquitted by a jury in November 1993. Lorena Bobbitt in turn was tried on charges that included malicious wounding, but a jury apparently bought her defense that she had snapped after being assaulted, and found her not guilty by reason of temporary insanity. Here Lorena Bobbitt should have been totally acquitted but it may have been a consolation to her since some form of leniency of this conviction did take place. Also were these problems of sexual assault about money where John Wayne Bobbitt honoured himself and lacked money or known in the Authorized King James Version Bible as "bread" where that here also it may have been possible that Lorena Bobbitt was making more money than him? Who as a man John Wayne Bobbitt wanted to honour himself by being in control of her by raping her because she had been making more money than him? By working as a cosmetologist and as a cosmetician and as well as being skilled in adornment and hair, nails, and complexion and making more of this money than him or as the Bible calls money " bread " here according to Proverbs 12: 7, 8, 9, 10 ? Here the term " beast " in Proverbs 12: 10 could refer to those who provide employment to John Wayne Bobbitt and monetary revenue or income from his job. So here also because of the many obvious reasons the couple eventually divorced in 1995.

When Robin Heidt started having an affair with her brother-in-law, Craig, she had no idea it would turn tragic. Shortly after her husband, Carey, found out about the affair, he was found gunned down in his home alongside with his parents. But as police searched the scene, they noticed right away that something wasn't right. The crime scene appeared to be staged to look like a break-in even though nothing was taken.
Friends and family grew suspicious when Craig moved into Robin's house

four months after the murders. He is living in his dead brother's house, sleeping in his dead brother's bed next to his dead brother's wife, "Prosecutor Michael Muldrew" said during the trial. He is taking his dead brother's children to school and he's driving his dead brother's truck. He has become for all practical purposes, Carey Heidt.

Craig was later arrested and charged with the murder of his brother and father and was sentenced to life in prison. However, many locals believed Robin Heidt should've been incarcerated and convicted as well, like Craig was. Many were convinced of her innocence, even though the widower turned on Craig and even testified against him in court. "When I looked at him, I just felt disgust," she said on 48 hours Mystery. "Disgust at the affair, disgust at him period. I wasn't comfortable with the relationship anymore. I realized there is this chance that he could have done this." In 2011, Robin was in the news again for threatening her new boyfriend's ex.

Here Robin Heidt may have been cunning in her approach in looking for a life of pleasure even to the point of betraying her own husband by having an affair with her husband's brother to enjoy a better life because she may have been not satisfied with her husband and may have found that her husband's brother may have been more handsome and possibly better in bed or she was having marital problems with her husband and wanted to get revenge on him. She may have even betrayed her husband's brother Craig in order to avoid a conviction to being an accessory to murder by testifying against Craig saying she was disgusted by him. She was also accused of threatening her new boyfriend's ex. and this is also the sign of a woman who seeks for a life having no conscience and who is foolish and clamorous and is simple and knows nothing and proclaiming insistently and noisily for what she selfishly desires according to Proverbs 9: 13, 14, 15, 16, 17, 18.

When Theresa Stone and her husband Randy joined New Hope Baptist Church, they became close friends with Pastor David Love. Of course, they had no idea exactly how close this " friendship "would blossom. Later, in 2010, Randy was found shot and killed at his insurance office. Shocked family and friends showed up to New Hope Baptist Church to light candles and listen to Pastor David Love's eulogy to his late friend. But right away, investigators were suspicious. When both David and Theresa were called in for questioning, police were skeptical of their tight alibis. When a torn-up letter was found in the pastor's office, investigators learned that Theresa and David were having an affair. She had given a gun to David in hope that with her husband out of the way, they could start a new life together.

David is currently serving a life sentence, and Theresa is serving an eight-year sentence for conspiracy to commit murder. As parishioners of a church what drove Pastor David Love and Theresa Stone to commit this murder? Perhaps it may have been a compatible life style that both Theresa Stone and David Love had together ---- that it provoked them to eliminate Theresa Stone's husband and in hopes of living a more pleasurable life. Here they were the members or the parishioners of a Baptist Church and were religiously apostate in nature according to 2nd Peter 2: 1, 2, 3.

In 2014, Sabrina Limon's husband, Robert, was found gunned down in the train yard where he worked. "We thank you all so much for acts of random kindness that has been shown to us " This was written in cold and cunningly and deceptive way on a post on Facebook after her husband's death." Flowers, gifts, hugs, Food. All of the love ---- love that has come to us has been such a beautiful tribute to the amazing man Robert was and will never be forgotten" Here this fair speech is also common among some of society's extroverts where a number of people are however subject to a will where there is a complete abomination in their hearts. Here in Biblical numerical symbolism the number " 7 " represents spiritual perfection and completion according to Proverbs 26: 25. Here an investigation revealed that it was actually Sabrina who was behind the murder, along with Jonathan Hearn her new lover.

During their trial, Jonathon testified that the two originally had planned to poison Robert by putting arsenic in banana pudding. However, fearing they would get caught. Sabrina called her husband and told him to throw the dessert away. They then chose a gun as their murder weapon hoping it would not trace back to them. Jonathan was later convicted and got a reduced sentence for testifying against his former lover. As for Sabrina, she's currently serving 25 years in prison. Here she may have been so selfish that it led to how simplistic and foolish and clamorous she was according to Proverbs 9: 13, 14, 15, 16, 17, 18.

Pamela Smart in 1990 shocked the world when her husband, Greggory, was found murdered. Although the public was originally sympathetic to the grieving widow, investigators quickly learned that not only was Pamela behind the murder, but she sought help from her 15-year-old student lover, William "Billy" Flynn. In order to avoid a pricey divorce and profit off her husband's life insurance policy, she asked Billy to kill her husband, threatening to withhold sex if he didn't. Here this conspiracy and whoredom and also of an imperious or domineering woman who had domineered William "Billy" Flynn is also mentioned in the Authorized King James Version Bible according to Ezekiel 16: 28, 29, 30, 31, 32, 33, 38. Here the husband paid by getting enticed by Pamela's beauty and was sexually tempted by getting involved with her and her imperious and domineering ways and paying with his death and in turn she payed for his murder or death she committed as this chapter's title is called "Retribution For Death," which has described this topic of this crime with such uncanny accuracy.

The case became a media sensation, inspiring the movie "To Die For" starring Nicole Kidman. Today, Billy has been released from prison after serving a 25-year sentence. Pamela is serving a life sentence and still claims she's innocent.

Feeling Bored with his life, Thomas Montgomery started chatting with a teenage girl he met in a chatroom named "Talhotblond." He lied to her and said he was 18 instead of 47. Together, the two had a cyber affair that lasted until Thomas' wife found out. Realizing he could no longer pursue the relationship anymore, Thomas told the truth to Talhotblond about his real age. Horrified, the teen turned her attention to Thomas' 22- year-old co-worker, Brian Barrett. As the two grew closer, Thomas became jealous.

In 2006, as Brian sat in his car, Thomas shot him with a sniper rifle. As investigators arrived at the scene and started questioning co-workers, they learned about the love triangle. Worried about Talhotblond's safety, police arrived at her home where they found Mary Shiele, a middle-aged mom. It turned out that Mary had been pretending to be her teenage daughter Jessi, (who was known as "Talhotblond" to Thomas) and "Talhotblond's" mother was catfishing the two men all along. Thomas is currently serving a 20-year sentence, and although Mary was never convicted of anything, her daughter and husband no longer speak to her. Here online messages that are sent quickly like lightnings is now deception that is now cunningly paramount with scams and even lying about your age where the term "we" or "here we are" refers to the fact that you do not know the person you are talking to or see what his or her appearance is like. Where if you know the person the term "Here I am" would be used instead of the term "Here we are" that is a description of online internet and online web activity and socialization where online users are not familiar with one another or not known to each other or do not know what they look like to each other as mentioned here by the Authorized King James Version Bible according to Job 38: 35 "Canst thou send lightnings, that they may go, and say unto thee, Here we are?"

In 2007, witnesses watched in horror as a masked woman shot Heather Garraus in the parking lot of a Credit Union. "You ruined my Life! Get on the ground," the gunman said before pulling the trigger. However, once officers were called on the scene, they quickly zeroed in on Shawna Nelson, a co-worker who had been having a public affair with Heather's husband, Ignacio. Not only did Ignacio father a baby with Shawna, he also tried to break up with Shawna numerous times throughout the tumultuous three-year affair. However, when Ignacio decided to end things for good. Shawna went off the deep end, shooting Heather in an act of revenge. Shawna was later convicted and sentenced to life in prison.

As for Ignacio, he takes full responsibility for the tragic love triangle he helped create. "Oh yes I loathe myself," Ignacio said in a televised NBC interview, "and I got to hide it so my kid doesn't see how bad I loathe myself. Because a beautiful woman's dead for me having an affair and the chain of events that I had no way of foreseeing. But ultimately if I never had an affair, Heather would be alive. It's on me."

Here the ways of a man seem right to him ---but in the end death approaches whether of himself or a of a friend or loved one. Here he had lost a friend and someone he loved dearly --- which was his wife. So, this love affair seemed right in Ignacio's eyes but in the end, it was the tragic murder and death of his wife according to Proverbs 16: 25. What was his Retribution For Death here? The fact that he has to live with this tragedy for the rest of his entire life. Knowing that his child which he loves will have to eventually get knowledge here of this affair he had that caused the death of his wife which he loved so dearly and that had become his child's mother's death as well.

In 2006, Els Clottemans and Els Van Doren went Skydiving with their instructor, Marcel Somers. Already there was tension amongst the threesome considering both women were vying for to challenge or to strive to date or to seek affection from Marcel Somers. Clottemans really started to feel unhinged when, while hanging out with Marcel and Van Doren, she heard the pair having sex. The following day on a skydiving expedition, Van Doren horrifically found that both her parachute and safety chute pull cords or the chute's cords themselves had been cut after leaving the plane moments later into the dive. Where she fell to her death. Police were instantly suspicious of Clottemans. When they called her in for questioning, she tried to commit suicide. Although the police didn't have solid evidence, they were certain she cut the cords and she was found guilty in court and she was sentenced to 30 years in prison in 2010. She still maintains her innocence.

Here the Retribution For Death is a price that is paid when we become too socially involved with the people around us that may question who we should trust? Life is not fair because we may have enemies in our own household or a close friend that is considered a sister. That this notion of believing that she may be a true sister, may not be the case, but someone who has the potential to plot harm or murder those of us who believe in the truth. And for those of us who despise their envy and jealousy since their anger and contention is for us to remain and dwell in the wilderness. And not seek that contention against your adversarial person or an adversarial woman's covetous and contentious ways. Here life is strange because we may have enemies or foes in our own household who may be considered to be a close friend or sister or brother or daughter or mother or father or son or relative etc. according to Proverbs 21: 19 and Matthew 10: 35, 36. Where in the end you could become subjected to trouble or harm or even death.

CHAPTER 5
DESPICABLE KILLER ON THE LOOSE

My books like "Pyromancy" and "Open Tomb, Aviation 666, Monsters of Genesis" and "Magistrates of Damnation" and "Immunity From Prosecution" and this book you are holding now called "Ancient Blood of Violence" may have caused the war in Ukraine and Israel and may have provoked those people who are anti-Semitic and that they want to wipe Israel off the map. Here since I represent someone who is a Christian and who believes in the God of Israel and the Authorized King James Version Bible. And the fact that I may be a servant of God after writing these 5 books. It may be obvious that this recent violence and war in the middle east and in Ukraine may have been caused by the dispute regarding religion and that these problems did take place since 1948 regarding Israel being established in having a homeland which was 12 years before I was born. But the recent violence may have been partially sparked by my books that I have written. Here the perpetrators of this violence and the ones who were responsible for the violence and the invasion of Ukraine by Russia and the attacks on Israel is that here Putin may have also orchestrated this attack on Israel for the purpose to create a distraction from the Ukraine war who these perpetrators were also bent on having me blamed for this war in Ukraine and the attacks on Israel and then have me contemned by having me brought upon the necks of the slain according to Ezekiel 21: 29.

Here the world will be convinced that I was to be blamed for this religious controversy that caused this Invasion in Ukraine and the Attacks on Israel where here I may be questioned by the world and it's ambassadors of all nations who believe that these atrocities should have not taken place had it not been for my books that I have written. And that I was considered rich because of my possible immortality that I may receive at the second coming of Christ ---- here this was their envy that was the similar envy the Pharisees and Authorities had in the time of Christ and of how they wanted to crucify him on a cross that same way they want to crucify me in a furnace. And that it is a divine lie to have me and every tree or person contemned who truly believes in Christ in order to secure their coming Global Babylonian One World Empire Government of excessive sex and excessive food and excessive materialism brought on by the Antichrist and by contemning me and the true Christians of the Authorized King James Version Bible to secure their coming Babylonian Empire of the Antichrist according to Matthew 27 : 11, 12, 13, 14, 15, 16, 17, 18, 19, 20, 21, 22, 23, 24, 25, 26 and Ezekiel 21: 9, 10, 11, 29 and 2nd Chronicles 32: 27, 28, 29, 30, 31. A fight here between good and evil known as the coming prophecy of Armageddon according to Revelation 16: 12, 13, 14, 15, 16 and Proverbs 29: 27.

We had many despicable killers on the loose in this world from the ancient period of Genesis to our present world we have today. But nothing has come close to a person named Vladimir Putin who has been a President of a country that has harboured political adversaries of God and the Bible. And that Vladimir Putin being a man who recruits these kinds of people, invaded a country like Ukraine without a cause and brought suffering and destruction without a justified cause to this semi -poor and peaceful country led by President Volodymyr Zelenskyy. Who was a President who displayed courage and unrelenting perseverance in the face of the Death and Destruction and Chaos that Vladimir Putin has caused. Not only to Ukraine but to the rest of the world.

This man Vladimir Putin has been a man who has caused more grief and sorrow and suffering and total chaos and destruction to not only Ukraine that suffered deadly casualties of this war and invasion by Putin and Russia's authoritarian leadership but brought the world to its knees with an economic burden to those who have limited revenue and income and to those in extreme poverty. Since he has taken the reigns of power in Russia since 1999 and as prime minister from 1999 to 2000 and President from 2000 to 2012 and remained in power as president of Russia since 2000 to the present at the time of this Writing of September 23 / 2023. Here Vladimir Putin has committed destruction and genocide without a cause. He is a man who was and is far worse and more shameful than Jeffrey

Dahmer, a notorious and sexual Necrophiliac. Who is mentioned in chapter 3 of this book where Jeffrey Dahmer was not as bad because he did not cause the suffering of millions upon millions of people worldwide inflicting depression and trauma and suffering and death so devastating that it caused families all around the world to subside in economic morass that has sunk the citizens of this global village of planet earth into extreme poverty.

And to question why this man Vladimir Putin is permitted to continue to rule a country in this world, much less be allowed to live? And not be held accountable for what he has done and not to be brought to justice in our world, is that even some of the worse dictators in this world may have questioned his motives for what he has perpetrated against Ukraine and this destruction and genocide he committed against the people of Ukraine without a justified cause during and by this invasion of Ukraine. And that if it wasn't for Volodymyr Zelenskyy and Justin Trudeau and Canada and Biden and the U.S. and Britain, that here we who are in this democratic part of this world would have been victims of this world by those who also rule this world who are the flipside to democracy that is ruled by dictators who are in congruity with Vladimir Putin. Here a politician like Zelenskyy is a man who the Bible calls "wise counsel" according to: Proverbs 24: 6 "For by wise counsel thou shalt make thy war; and in multitude of counsellors there is safety."

Here the total Civilian casualties From February 24th / 2022, which marked the start of the large-scale armed attack by the Russian Federation, to September 10th / 2023. Here the Office of the High Commissioner for Human Rights (OHCHR) recorded 27, 149 civilian casualties in the country of Ukraine that was numbered at 9,614 that were killed and 17, 535 that were injured. And as of August 18th / 2023 one document said that as of February Ukraine's military war casualties had suffered 124, 500 to 131,000 casualties, with as many as 17,500 killed in action.

Here all these casualties of civilians and of Ukraine's military was unfortunately inevitable as Zenlenskyy did what any wise leader would do and that is to avoid to attack Russian territory in the beginning of this war and during the mid-period of this war. Here it made him less culpable to the United Nations and NATO for trying to avoid unnecessary casualties of innocent Russian Civilians placing Putin in a bad position and political light. Throwing him into darkness and appearing as a cruel dictator to his own people while Zelenskyy 's political reputation as a strong and just leader of Ukraine and the rest of the world has secured his political position in the world that has awarded him to be in a favorable position among not only the leaders of democracy in this world but to some of the authoritarian leaders and regimes in our world. Where not even Kevin McCarthy who like some Republicans that has envy towards Zelenskyy like those Pharisees who were the authorities at the time of Christ who had envy towards Christ as well where they released a robber and a possible murderer and had Christ crucified without a cause in place of this murderer. Here Kevin Mcarthy would not acknowledge Zelenskyy; but having envy towards Zelenskyy who put up a good fight in this war humiliating Putin and all those Republicans that favor Trump and dictators around the world like Putin during this unjust invasion and war in Ukraine.

Here House speaker Kevin McCarthy Republican of California, said he has questions for the Ukrainian president when asked if he plans to commit to another round of aid. Here Kevin McCarthy with envy according to Matthew 27: 11, 12, 13, 14 ,15 ,16 ,17, 18, 19 ,20, 21, 22, 23 ,24, 25, 26 says quote to ABC news Senior Congressional Correspondent Rachel Scott; "Where's the accountability on the money we've already spent? What is the plan for victory? I think that's what the American public wants to know," said McCarthy.

Here Kevin McCarthy shows how he favors a dictatorship mindset --- because only those who support Putin directly; or indirectly like Kevin McCarthy has done and has been doing and will do in the future are the ones who favor a tyrannical government. That dictates to the populace to extreme measures as to have absolute control in order for the elite to prosper excessively and enslave the rest of humanity in this coming one world Government worldwide and developing and having an apostate religious and economic order consisting of digital and artificial Intelligence perpetrated by the Antichrist as mentioned in the Authorized King James Version Bible in the book of Revelation in Chapters 17 and 18 and Revelation 13: 14, 15, 16, 17, 18.

Here the White house has asked for an additional 24 Billion dollars to support Ukraine in its fight against Russia's invaders-- a request backed by congressional Democrats. Senate Republican leader Mitch McConnell, Republican of Kentucky, has publicly advocated for continued defense and financial assistance. But McCarthy is more skeptical, and a growing number of House Republican hard-liners are adamantly opposed to sending more money to the war-torn nation. McCarthy has repeatedly said that the United States should not be giving Ukraine a "blank check" though has vehemently criticized Russia's actions. Look what Russia has done -- invade --- is wrong. McCarthy said also that it is an atrocity,---- we want to make sure that ends. I also have always said from the beginning, no matter what the issue is, I want accountability for whatever the hardworking taxpayers spend their money on. I want to plan for a victory. So no, I will listen to the American public. I will follow what happens in Congress, but I will have questions for president Zelensky. "

I John Bazzanella the author of this book believes that this is utter bullshit and lies by Kevin McCarthy. This war in Ukraine is that propaganda is being used here to get Trump elected in 2024. And make it appear that Trump solves the Middle East problems. Like the attack on Israel that has happened recently on Saturday October 7th / 2023 and terrorism and the invasion of Ukraine that led to the war that started on February 24th / 2022. Here after Donald Trump gets elected this war in Ukraine which was propagated will end. After Trump is elected, and after his election and is back in the office of the presidency of the United States Vladimir Putin will certainly co- operate with Trump and end the war in Ukraine giving Trump that momentum in his position as president of the United States. And propagate his potential for worldwide leadership flattering his voters and the rest of the world who are demanding efforts to end the war in Ukraine.

By making it appear like he has ended the war in Ukraine making him a hero in the sight of humanity. And to make it appear by this propagation that the Republicans are peace makers instead of tyrants. Where here after they deceive the world populace in each and every country worldwide and get a man like Donald Trump elected who favors dictators in the world. That here after these Republicans turn the country of the U.S. and every other country in the world under the same or similar influence of the political conditions that become embedded in authoritarianism worldwide in each and every country in the world. Then the world will then witness when it is too late that Donald Trump and those of his Republicans and their true intentions of tyrannical rule and dictatorship will be slaughtering millions worldwide who refuse to worship their evil One world Government Empire of the Antichrist or Beast and refuse to accept this digital one world currency or known as the Mark of the Beast which the Bible warns of eternal damnation for worshipping their One World Government Empire of this Beast or Antichrist Government and accepting this one world currency known as the Mark of the Beast, according to Revelation 14: 9, 10, 11.

Here Kevin McCarthy is pulling the wool over the eyes of those who support him and Donald Trump and those Republicans who favor Donald Trump. Here it is all about winning people over by expressing cunningly the disapproval of the invasion and war perpetrated by Russia. Here there is a conspiracy to give an upper edge or advantage to the dictators of this world to put forth a semi Democratic and semi Republican one world government regime that will have a diplomatic tyrannical feel to it where here this conspiracy is to deceive the populace of every nation on earth and use the war in Ukraine as propaganda as a leverage here that is meant to make the war continue until Trump who will be elected according to the statistics and polls that favor him as the presidential candidate to win the election in in 2024. And when he does take office, the Republicans along with Putin and other dictators around the world will make it appear as if Donald Trump has solved and ended the war in Ukraine and make it appear like he has also solved the middle east problems as well.

Here they will claim that Donald Trump is a trustworthy worldwide political leader that will even solve the financial woes of the worldwide economy; as this deception will be paramount to win these people or populace of every country on planet earth to deceive those who have or will reject the word of God and the Biblical prophecies that have been fulfilled. And to execute a sentence of death through a diplomatically and humane and in a peaceful way by a guillotine in every community courtroom in each and every district in each and every country worldwide of all those who refuse to worship this One World Government of the Antichrist or Beast who have their faith in God and in Christ. And also, of those who are taking heed to the prophetic warnings of being subject to eternal condemnation to damnation by God and as mentioned in the Authorized Kings James Version Bible. That here if they worship this One world Government leader or tyrant known and mentioned in the Bible as the Antichrist or Beast they will be condemned to damnation and if they refuse to worship this one world government of the Antichrist or Beast they will be become martyrs for Christ receiving eternal life in heaven according to Revelation 13: 14, 15,16, 17, 18 and Revelation 14: 9, 10, 11 and Revelation 20: 4 and Revelation 6: 9, 10, 11 and Daniel 8: 25 and Revelation 20: 12, 13, 14, 15.

Here Zelenskyy was able to secure more funding -- 50 billion dollars -- when he last was in Washington. The dramatic visit made last December which was his first visit which was the first known trip outside of Ukraine since the war began. Speaking to a packed joint session of Congress Zelenskyy delivered a plea for additional help with weapons and financial assistance. He told lawmakers the "money is not charity."

Here this money is not a gift or charity Since Zelenskyy hates gifts. As this contribution of funds brings the world perhaps to a better place since to establish the multitude counsels of peace and not war can be easily disappointed if the dictators of this world get their way. Bringing a tyrannical multitude of counsellors to these world regimes that harbour dictators who may take control of and enslave the peaceful process of democracy and disappointing the establishment of counsellors of democracy and having or being without counsel purposes to execute peace and prosperity for all of humanity according to: Proverbs 15: 22, 23, 24, 25,

26, 27 "Without counsel purposes are disappointed: but in the multitude of counselors they are established. A man hath joy by the answer of his mouth: and a word spoken in due season, how good is it! The way of life is above to the wise, that he may depart from hell beneath. The Lord will destroy the house of the proud: but he will establish the border of the widow. The thoughts of the wicked are an abomination to the Lord: but the words of the pure are pleasant words. He that is greedy of gain troubleth his own house: but he that hateth gifts shall live."

CHAPTER 6
FUTURE BLOOD OF VIOLENCE

What is this future blood of violence? Today we have violence that is spreading and infiltrating communities with gun violence, stabbings, and in some rare cases vehicle homicides. Our world's population is increasing and causing the depletion of land to build housing for people who don't have a place to live who have a low income. Low income individuals have a hard time accessing and securing a place to live because of the huge demand for housing. Here the price of rent has sky rocketed at the time of this writing of September 25th / 2023 in the city of Toronto and perhaps in other cities across North America and in other parts of the world. The fact that the population has increased it has brought the statistics to violence to a new high.

The reason for this violence is the fact that most people are in poverty and are unable to secure a place to live like an apartment leaving these people homeless without a fixed address and therefore are unable to find employment because of not possessing a fixed address. This type of situation leaves society and individuals open to the prospect of joining gangs and taking part in becoming drug dealers on the street and even spending money on drugs for not only to sell on the street but to also use the drugs themselves that cause them to become addicted and in some cases they may even be subject to an overdose leading to needing medical assistance putting a huge load and demand on the Health Care System.

Here this problem has been compounded by others who have suffered from violent incidents such as gunshot wounds, or stabbings, or subject to an illness like sexually transmitted diseases and commonly rare diseases that sweep through populations like Cancer, Heart disease, etc., or dementia, which cost the government millions of dollars or will cost the Government billions of dollars in the not too distant future, now that dementia and the people getting this these types of diseases is now on the rise with an aging population derived from the baby boomer generation and the rejection of Christ and eating excessively and having multiple sex partners or committing sexual immorality or fornication and corrupting the flesh with disease and sickness according to Galatian 6: 7, 8. Here it will be leading to costing the governments of the world billions of dollars in Health Care and taking care of those who have these diseases of dementia who are frail and not able to take care of themselves or not able to house themselves who are also near to eventual death. Someone in the world develops dementia every 3 seconds. There are over 55 million people worldwide living with dementia in 2020. This number will almost double every 20 years, reaching 78 million in 2030 and 139 million in 2050. Much of the increase will be in developing countries.

Also, alcohol poisoning affecting kidney and liver functions is also causing a financial burden on Health Care. Also smoking that has led to lung cancer costing the Government's Health Care System billions of dollars to provide treatment for all these disease stricken people and which also includes injuries because of gun violence and other violent incidents such as assaults and the occurrences of also the rare terrorism involving rare vehicular homicides which also includes car accidents which are an everyday occurrence. And also the common occurrence of terrorism of mass shootings in schools and malls and events in the communities. And another common occurrence involving terrorism is the copycat incidents that have taken place involving mass shootings in schools and malls and events in the communities. Also, road rage has also been on the increase a sign that any incident whether small or great participates in the last days of these dangerous and perilous times now occurring on planet earth according to 2nd Timothy 3: 1, 2, 3, 4, 5.

Here money is an economic burden that only corrupts man's prosperity which is the root of all evil. Here we are sinking into an economic morass where the leaders of the Babylonian lifestyle want to use these digital online transactions that are prone at times to failures regarding executing these electronic transactions to purchase different types of items and commodities where the world economy depends on this digital technology. Here the world wants to get rid of the transaction of money or paper currencies worldwide because of the enormous potential for fraud and scams. Well this digital online technology to improve the elimination of scams regarding bad checks and phony paper currencies has made matters even worse and backfired by switching to online digital transactions where individual victims alone were taken for hundreds of thousands of dollars and even in some cases close to a million dollars of their life savings being scammed online. And these scams happen daily and on an enormous worldwide scale costing innocent and vulnerable victims billions of dollars every year since these online digital transactions began to take place within the last 20 years or so.

 Here people refuse to give up using their money and convert to the Barter System worldwide. Here the Barter system makes scams and fraud fool proof unless citizens don't show up for work. Where here in this system rations would be put in place. And the Justice System would get involved deeply in this Barter System making sure that the rations of the wealth of these commodities be distributed to the global citizens fairly and evenly and that the justice system would be making sure citizens would show up for work unless they are having health problems.

Also CNN at the time of writing here on September 26th / 2023 has said that Putin has experienced a humiliating set -back in this war against Ukraine but is now gaining some ground and that the west is not willing to suffer like these countries who have these dictators like Putin of Russia or like Xi Jinping of China or other dictators like Kim Jong Un of North Korea etc. ---- we also have Saudi Arabia's Mohammed bin Salman another dictator where here the balance of power between the democratic world and the authoritarian world is at best now close to 50 / 50. But this will eventually change if the citizens of the west are not willing to give up their prosperity and their millions of dollars in their bank accounts to fight this war in Ukraine where eventually Putin and other dictators alike who will infiltrate the U.S. politically by a man we know as Donald Trump who will be elected in 2024.

Also, in the House of Commons in Ottawa a visit by Ukrainian President Volodymr Zelenskyy was marred when Yaroslav Hunka a former Nazi received a standing ovation in the House of Commons as a war hero but was soon discovered that he was a former Nazi. A Russian embassy account posted online that Ukraine was issuing stamps with the face of Yaroslav Hunka, who received a standing ovation in the House of Commons before it was revealed he served in a Nazi unit during the Second World War. This stamp had Yaroslav Hunka's updated picture of his face with the quote "Heroes Don't Die." Was this Propaganda of Yaroslav Hunka? A former Nazi that was planned and that infiltrated the Canadian Government? And that the House of Commons speaker Anthony Rota who may have been deceived and that Yaroslav Hunka was invited to attend that visit and speech made by Vorodymyr Zelenskyy? And then it was revealed that he served in a Nazi unit for Ukraine in the Second World War? To make it appear like Putin has a genuine disapproval of Nazi's? Giving Putin this credit that his scheme is genuine and not just propaganda and to make it appear like the Canadian Government is discredited and that the west cannot be trusted?

People in the west who will not listen to Vorodymyr Zelenskyy will have a dictatorship on their doorstep sometime in the near future if they want to save their money and not help Ukraine in this war and would either by complying with this dictatorship end up in hell for worshipping this worldwide dictatorial regime; or end up seriously injured of tortured or dead like those Ukrainian citizens who became causalities in this war in Ukraine and being martyrs for Christ according to Revelation 20: 4 and Revelation 6: 9, 10, 11.

Here all of these dictators along with Donald Trump will bring on a Tyrannical One World Government where eventually the west would have to submit to a worldwide authoritarian rule that will turn to a cruel tyrannical regime in the end and have 10 global contributing dictators or kings to bring about a worldwide regime under the rule of one man which would be known in the Bible as the Beast or Antichrist. And these 10 dictators will give and submit their power to this Beast or Antichrist according to Revelation 17: 12, 13, and committing worldwide genocide of true Christians and their converts of the Authorized King James Version Bible according to Revelation 20: 4 and Revelation 6: 9, 10, 11.

 And yes, in the end the west and the rest of the world will accept this Beast or a man like Donald Trump according to John 5: 43 and who owns Estate and Towers according to Daniel 11: 21 and which the term "estate" in Daniel 11: 21 refers to a "pedestal" or "station." "And the children of Israel did secretly those things that were not right against the Lord their God and they built them high places in all their cities from the tower of the watchmen to the fenced city" that these things are mentioned here in # 3653 and same as # 3651 of the Old Testament of the "The New Strong's Expanded Exhaustive Concordance of the Bible". Here they will accept this Beast or Antichrist because money and peace and prosperity are something, they or the Babylonian lifestyle here craves which is this excessive sex and excessive food and excessive materialism.

And that also here they will depend on this false peace and money and prosperity promised by Donald Trump and will accept him as a leader and saviour to the world after he ends this war in Ukraine and drastically improves the worldwide economy by a one world digital currency known as the Mark of the Beast mentioned in Revelation 13: 14, 15, 16, 17, 18. And in the end the world will be deceived. And if it were possible to even deceive the very elect servants of God according to Matthew 24: 24, and reject a man of the Bible who we know as Jesus Christ who died on that cross 2,000 years ago. And then the world goes about to accept a man who comes in his own name who may very well be Donald Trump who promises peace and prosperity and safety and in this process of promising this peace and prosperity and safety deceives the whole world in the end that leads to false religion and conflict that leads to war and eventual destruction where Donald Trump shall come to his end and where his dictatorship and worldwide empire and regime ends and where a possible furnace regicide by a Servant of God takes place as well according to John 5: 41, 42, 43, 44, and 1st Thessalonians 5: 3 and Daniel 7: 11 and Daniel 11: 43, 44, 45 and Psalms 136: 17, 18 and Jeremiah 15: 14, 19, 20, 21. How does this Servant of God regicide this Beast or Antichrist ? The Antichrist finances to build a furnace to sentence this servant of God and this plan may backfire according to Esther 7: 9, 10. There are some of us who suffered and spoke good for our King " The Lord Jesus Christ." I say to Donald Trump? Do you really want to build that furnace? But keep in mind 2nd Peter 1: 20! This goes for those of us who place their trust in God and the Lord Jesus Christ of the Authorized King James Version Bible and for those who are against God and the Lord Jesus Christ of the Authorized King James Version Bible.

EPILOGUE

This ancient blood of violence that our world has experienced since the time of Genesis has definitely made us think of violence as a common occurrence; so much so that it is not dealt with appropriately in most parts of the world. The regimes that do deal with violent offenders are indeed the ones who make the laws that deal with violence appropriately but are violent extremists who are prone to excessive violence and that are law breakers themselves and violating human rights. Violence has plagued humanity down through the centuries to this recent period in history. Like the 911 terrorist attack on the World Trade Center that happened because man was greedy and had an envious approach toward being in poverty while watching others prosper in peace and health and the enormous wealth they managed to attain.

The Neanderthal may have been a variant specie of homo sapiens that was caught up and prone to violence. Who knows what type of specie of humanity or different entities of humans may have existed before or during the time of Adam and Eve. Or if during the period of Adam and Eve the visitation of the Sons of God on this planet may have put some sort of monkey wrench into this civilization to make it go so bad that violence erupted to the point of excessive blood and mutilation that because it was so perverted that sexual immorality took part also in these sins that were so vile that sex was view upon as a sign of shame and disgust by us all. That humanity had carried on with having this reputation of being the lowest form of man or being compared to being lower completely than any extraterrestrial entity out of this world.

Or in the far unreachable parts of the Universe that in the beginning of Genesis that the Sons of God had infiltrated this planet with this mating with the daughters of men on this planet that brought offsprings of deformities of Giants and deformities of the flesh in humans. And this depravity that brought my loss of all my royalties without a cause to all my books that I had written and paid for to get published (according to Isaiah 39 and Psalms 69: 4) and the scams and fraud and deceit that the rest of us who may have also experienced and coupled with these sins of fraudulent scams and deceit is this sexually vile and depraved humanistic behaviour of sin, is this violence that infiltrated evil into the imagination and characteristic will of man's sins and to this planet affecting also the prosperity and safety of Police officers, Judges, Aviation pilots, Emergency Personnel like Firefighters and paramedics and the Military personnel and soldiers of peace keeping missions and of war in a prudent and life preserving way avoiding the loss of innocent victims in the casualties and blunders of war, according to Proverbs 24: 6.

That here they have been also victims of friendly fire. And also aviation pilots that are risking flights that are plagued by the risks of terrorism or a troubling aviation aircraft maintenance industry and the death of passengers and pilots in these aviation disasters plagued by faulty maintenance and terrorism who are scattered into the corners of remembrance and resulting in this remembrance to cease from among men according to Deuteronomy 32: 25, 26, 27, 28, 29, 30, 31. Here because of a depressing economic situation the world finds itself in and working tirelessly being victims of exhaustion into this decade of enormous inflation and increased flight population. And to risk these flights for a multitude of passengers worldwide who need to arrive to their destinations to see their loved ones where violence and fraud and deception in our world had plagued humanity and all of us from the very beginning according Genesis 6: 1, 2, 3, 4, 5.

CREDITS AND ACKNOWLEDGEMENTS

I would to thank God and our Lord and Saviour Jesus Christ and for the divine Authorized Kings James Version Bible and I also like to thank James Strong L.L.D., S.T.D. for "The Strong's Expanded Exhaustive Concordance of the Bible." I would also like to thank "The University of Waikato" and Gabbi Shaw of the "Insider" and "Wikipedia" as well.

I would also like to thank all of my publishers like Dorrance Publishing who gave me the start in publishing with my first book called "Pyromancy" which did reject my second and third and fourth and fifth book and refused to help me get my second book published; where I was given that second chance by Kate Rodriguez to publish my second book called "Open Tomb, Aviation 666, Monsters of Genesis," and my third book called "Magistrates of Damnation" and my fourth book called "Immunity from Prosecution" that is in the process of being published at the time of this writing here of September 28th / 2023 by Kate Rodriguez and One Creative Media Publishing. I would like to thank her and One Media Creative Publishing for their efforts and the chance for this opportunity to have had these books and this coming fifth book called "Ancient Blood of Violence" to get published. Where even although I have paid to have these books published and although I am not receiving any royalties to any of my books here ---- these books being published have given me the opportunity for something viable for my job resume'.

 I would also like to Include thanking all of the following: "History Hit" "Britannica" "history.com; editors" "ABC News" "Kaushik Patowary --- Amusing Planet" "Journal Article" "Tiffany White" "Carlos Lozano --- L.A. Times".

And I would also like to express my sincere firm gratitude to the many other documented sources that I may have not mentioned; for if, it was not for all these Journalists, Editors, and Reporters and Documentarians, this book would have been impossible to accomplish or complete without their help and access to the history of forensics and crime and medical data and political stories and all their sources that has brought this book to an easy task and form of accomplishment and completion. .... AND LASTLY THE INSPIRATION AND HEART-BREAKING WRITING OF THE MUSCIANS OF "ASIA."

To the memory of the victims on both sides of these conflicts of Israel and Ukraine and the indigenous children who were the victims of a world gone insane............ February 24 / 2022.............. September 29th / 2023 .... October 7th / 2023 .... November 11th / 2023...

WILDEST DREAMS

They decorated all the generals
Who fought the war behind the lines
They had forgotten all the soldiers
The Brandy puts them way behind the times
Insanity has found its way to TV screens
Visions seems impossible to me
They fight (they fight) for king (for king) and country
I never would have thought this in my
Wildest dreams
Wildest dreams
Wildest dreams
Wildest dreams
The evening comes, we sit and watch the VJ's
Clips and rushes come from who knows where
From Washington across to California
With fighting breaking out in Leicester Square
We see the soldiers moving on to victory

And children trampled under marching feet
They fight (they fight) for king (for king) and country
How many millions will they put to sleep?
Wildest dreams
Wildest dreams
Wildest dreams
Wildest dreams
Fly away ....
No, not in this world
No, not in the next
No, not in my wildest dreams
They recommend euthanasia
For non- conformists anywhere
Some men's dreams for others turn to nightmares
This never would have happened in their
Wildest dreams
Wildest dreams
Wildest dreams
Wildest dreams
Fly away ....
No, not in this world
No, not in the next
No, not in my wildest dreams....................................

BY THE MUSICIANS OF " ASIA "
Sunday October 15th / 2023